W9-ASP-236

HISTORICAL ATLAS
OF THE WORLD

Barnes & Noble Books
A Division of Harper & Row, Publishers
New York, Hagerstown, San Francisco, London

This edition © Barnes & Noble Inc., New York
and
W. & R. Chambers Ltd., Edinburgh 1970

Latest Reprint 1977

Original edition © J. W. Cappelens Forlag A/S
Oslo 1962

The original Norwegian edition was prepared by
Oddvar Bjørklund, Haakon Holmboe and Anders Røhr
with maps by Berit Lie.

SBN: 06–463249–0 (paper)
06–490435–0 (cloth)

The publishers wish to record their gratitude to Haakon and Lotte
Holmboe, who cooperated in the preparation of this edition, and
to many teachers and lecturers in history who gave advice.

Library of Congress Catalog Card Number 78-80004

Printed in Scotland by John Bartholomew & Son Ltd, Edinburgh

FOREWORD

This *Historical Atlas of the World* has been designed for students in schools and universities—and anyone interested in history. It is informative and reliable yet attractively clear and handy to use.

The obvious aim is to illustrate history with the help of maps. The particular aim is not simply to localize past events geographically but to show the dynamic, the movement and the progress of history—the growth and decline of empires; the migration of races and nations; the encroachment of conquerors and the course of wars; the shifting of national boundaries; the fluctuating power structures between nations or religions; the growth of cultural and political movements— and much more. On several pages a number of individual maps, linked by a main theme, illustrate specific cultural and political developments.

Here, then, is history projected in maps instead of the written word—and maps such as these can fire the imagination as well.

CONTENTS   ANCIENT TIMES
From the dawn of civilization to the
time of the Roman emperors
Maps 1 to 31

CONTENTS THE MIDDLE AGES
From the Barbarian migrations to
the great voyages of discovery
Maps 32 to 55

CONTENTS   RECENT TIMES
From Charles V to Bismarck
Maps 56 to 93

CONTENTS   THE TWENTIETH CENTURY
From the Boer War to the present day
Maps 94 to 108

ABBREVIATIONS

AB.	Archbishopric
A.D.	Archduchy
B.	Bishopric
C.	County
c.	*circa*
D.	Duchy
Dsp.	Despotate
EL.	Electorate
exp.	expedition
G.D.	Grand Duchy
I., Is.	Island(s)
K.	Kingdom
LG.	Landgraviate
MG.	Margraviate
mod	modern name
Mt., Mts.	Mount, Mountain(s)
Pr.	Principality
Prov.	Province
Rep.	Republic

Index   follows Map 108

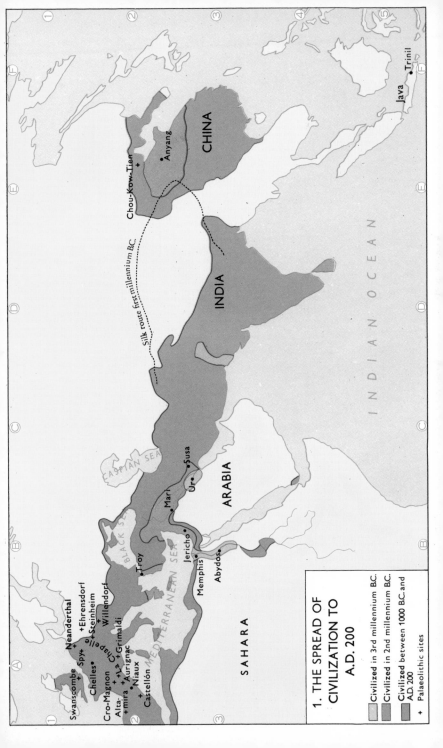

1. THE SPREAD OF
CIVILIZATION TO
A.D. 200

Civilized in 3-rd millennium B.C.

Civilized in 2nd millennium B.C.

Civilized between 1000 B.C. and
A.D. 200

+ Palaeolithic sites

CHINA

Chou-Kow-Tien

+ · Anyang

Silk route first millennium B.C.

INDIA

INDIAN OCEAN

Java

Trinil

CASPIAN SEA

Susa

Mari

Ur

ARABIA

BLACK S.

Troy

Jericho

Memphis

Abydos

MEDITERRANEAN SEA

SAHARA

Neanderthal

Swanscombe

Spy+

Chelles·

+Ehrensdorf

+Steinheim

Willendorf

Cro-Magnon

Alta-   +la + Grimaldi

+mira Aurignac

Niaux

Castellón

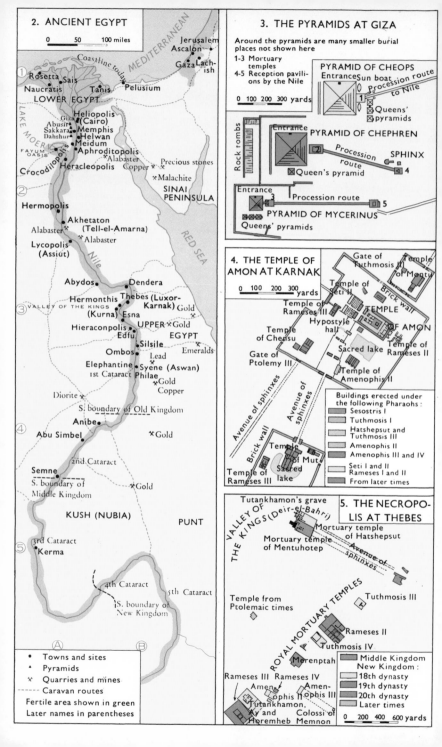

2. ANCIENT EGYPT

0   50   100 miles

MEDITERRANEAN

Coastline today

Jerusalem
Ascalon
Gaza Lachish

Rosetta
Sais
Naucratis
Tanis
Pelusium

LOWER EGYPT

LAKE MOERIS

Heliopolis
(Cairo)
Abusir
Sakkara
Memphis
Dahshur
Helwan
Meidum
FAYUM
OASIS
Aphroditopolis
Crocodilopolis
Heracleopolis

Alabaster
Copper
Precious stones

Malachite

SINAI
PENINSULA

RED SEA

Hermopolis

Akhetaton
(Tell-el-Amarna)
Alabaster
Alabaster
Lycopolis
(Assiút)

Abydos
Dendera

Hermonthis
Thebes (Luxor-
Karnak)
(Kurna)
Esna
Gold

VALLEY OF THE KINGS

Hieraconpolis
Edfu
UPPER
Gold
Silsile
EGYPT
Ombos
Lead
Emeralds
Elephantine
Syene (Aswan)
1st Cataract
Philae
Gold
Copper

Diorite

S. boundary of Old Kingdom

Anibe
Gold

Abu Simbel

2nd Cataract

Semne
S. boundary of
Middle Kingdom
Gold

KUSH (NUBIA)

PUNT

3rd Cataract
Kerma

4th Cataract
5th Cataract
S. boundary of
New Kingdom

● Towns and sites
▲ Pyramids
✕ Quarries and mines
--- Caravan routes
Fertile area shown in green
Later names in parentheses

3. THE PYRAMIDS AT GIZA

Around the pyramids are many smaller burial
places not shown here
1-3 Mortuary
temples
4-5 Reception pavili-
ons by the Nile

0   100   200   300 yards

PYRAMID OF CHEOPS

Entrance Sun boat
Procession route
to Nile
1
Queens'
pyramids

Rock tombs

Entrance
PYRAMID OF CHEPHREN
2
Procession
route
SPHINX
Queen's pyramid
4

Entrance
3
Procession route
5
PYRAMID OF MYCERINUS
Queens' pyramids

4. THE TEMPLE OF AMON AT KARNAK

0   100   200   300 yards

Gate of
Tuthmosis III
Temple
of Montu
Temple of
Seti II
Brick wall

Temple of
Rameses III
TEMPLE

Hypostyle
hall
OF AMON

Temple
of Chensu
Temple of
Rameses II

Sacred lake

Temple of
Amenophis II
Gate of
Ptolemy III

Temple of
Amenophis II

Buildings erected under
the following Pharaohs:
Sesostris I
Tuthmosis I
Hatshepsut and
Tuthmosis III
Amenophis II
Amenophis III and IV
Seti I and II
Rameses I and II
From later times

Avenue of sphinxes
Avenue of sphinxes
Brick wall

Temple
of Mut
Sacred
lake
Temple of
Rameses III

5. THE NECROPO-
LIS AT THEBES

Tutankhamon's grave
VALLEY OF
THE KINGS (Deir-el-Bahri)
Mortuary temple
of Hatshepsut
Mortuary temple
of Mentuhotep
Avenue of
sphinxes

Temple from
Ptolemaic times
Tuthmosis III

ROYAL MORTUARY TEMPLES

Rameses II
Tuthmosis IV
Merenptah

Rameses III Rameses IV
Amen-
ophis II
Amen-
ophis III
Tutankhamon,
Ay and
Horemheb
Colossi of
Memnon

Middle Kingdom
New Kingdom:
18th dynasty
19th dynasty
20th dynasty
Later times

0   200   400   600 yards

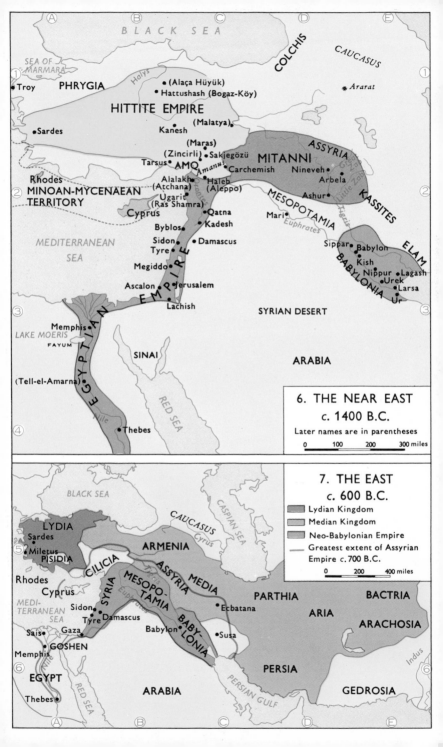

6. THE NEAR EAST
c. 1400 B.C.

Later names are in parentheses

0 — 100 — 200 — 300 miles

7. THE EAST
c. 600 B.C.

- Lydian Kingdom
- Median Kingdom
- Neo-Babylonian Empire
- Greatest extent of Assyrian Empire *c.* 700 B.C.

0 — 200 — 400 miles

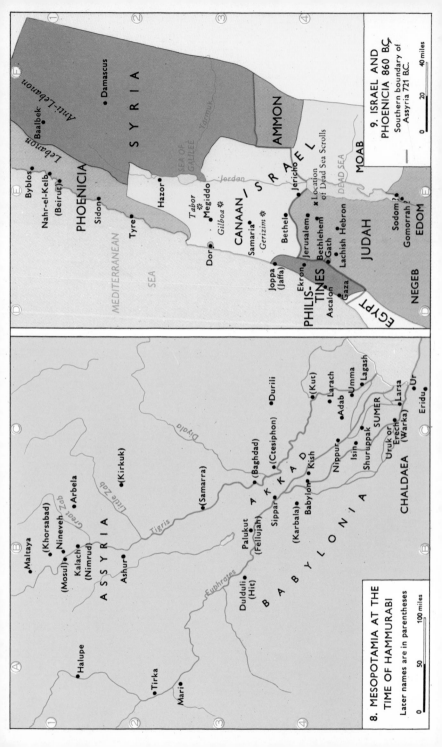

8. MESOPOTAMIA AT THE TIME OF HAMMURABI

Later names are in parentheses

0   50   100 miles

---

9. ISRAEL AND PHOENICIA 860 B.C.

Southern boundary of Assyria 721 B.C.

0   20   40 miles

Map 8 (Mesopotamia):

Halupe
Tirka
Mari
Dulduli (Hit)
Ashur
Palukut (Fellujah)
(Samarra)
Maltaya
(Khorsabad)
Nineveh (Mosul)
Kalach (Nimrud)
Arbela
(Kirkuk)
Sippar
(Karbala)
Babylon
(Baghdad)
(Ctesiphon)
Durili
Kish
Nippur
Isin
Shuruppak
Adab
(Kut)
Larach
Umma
Lagash
Uruk or Erech (Warka)
Larsa
Ur
Eridu

ASSYRIA
BABYLONIA
AKKAD
SUMER
CHALDAEA

Rivers: Euphrates, Tigris, Diyala, Great Zab, Little Zab

Map 9 (Israel and Phoenicia):

Byblos
Baalbek
Nahr-el-Kelb (Beirut)
Sidon
Tyre
Damascus
Hazor
Dor
Tabor
Megiddo
Gilboa
Samaria
Gerizim
Bethel
Joppa (Jaffa)
Jerusalem
Bethlehem
Ekron
Ascalon
Gaza
Gath
Jericho
Lachish Hebron
Sodom?
Gomorrah?

PHOENICIA
SYRIA
CANAAN
ISRAEL
AMMON
MOAB
JUDAH
EDOM
NEGEB
PHILIS-TINES
EGYPT

MEDITERRANEAN SEA
SEA OF GALILEE
DEAD SEA
Lebanon
Anti-Lebanon

x Location of Dead Sea Scrolls

Rivers: Jordan, Yarmuk

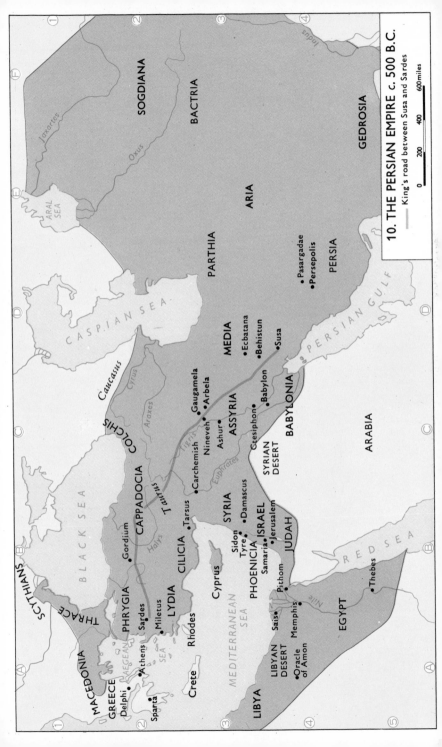

10. THE PERSIAN EMPIRE c. 500 B.C.

— King's road between Susa and Sardes

0   200   400   600 miles

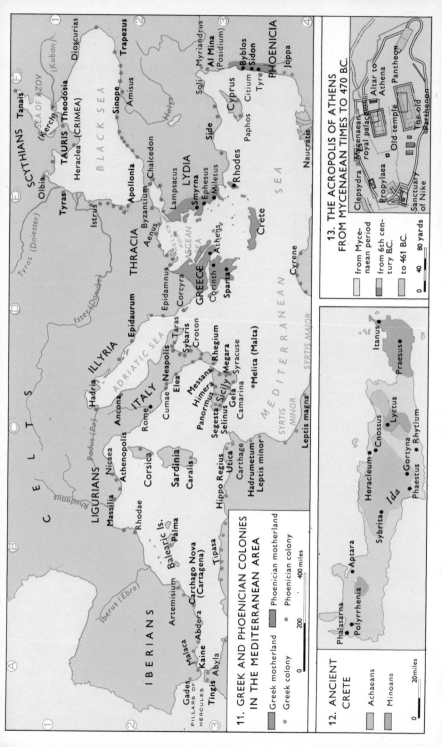

11. GREEK AND PHOENICIAN COLONIES IN THE MEDITERRANEAN AREA

Greek motherland
Greek colony
Phoenician motherland
Phoenician colony

0   200   400 miles

IBERIANS
Gades
PILLARS OF HERCULES
Malaca
Kaine
Abdera
Tingis Abyla
Artemisium
Massilia
Rhodae
Nicaea
Athenopolis
Balearic Is.
Palma
Carthago Nova (Cartagena)
Tipasa
Corsica
Sardinia
Caralis
Hippo Regius
Utica
Carthage
Hadrumetum
Leptis minor
Leptis magna
LIGURIANS
Rome
Cumae
Neapolis
Elea
Ancona
Hadria
ITALY
Taras
Sybaris
Croton
Rhegium
Messana
Himera
Panormus
Segesta
Selinus
Sicily
Gela
Camarina
Syracuse
Megara
Melita (Malta)
ILLYRIA
Epidamnus
Epidaurum
Corcyra
GREECE
Corinth
Athens
Sparta
Crete
Cyrene
CELTS
Rhodanus
Podus (Po)
ADRIATIC SEA
MEDITERRANEAN SEA
SYRTIS MINOR
SYRTIS MAJOR
Iberus (Ebro)
Tyras (Dniester)
Ister (Danube)

SCYTHIANS
Olbia
Tyras
Istrus
Tanais
(Kuban)
SEA OF AZOV (Kerch)
TAURIS (CRIMEA)
Theodosia
Heraclea
Dioscurias
Trapezus
Sinope
Amisus
Apollonia
Chalcedon
Byzantium
Lampsacus
Aenus
THRACIA
BLACK SEA
AEGEAN SEA
Halys
LYDIA
Smyrna
Ephesus
Miletus
Rhodes
Cyprus
Paphos
Side
Soli
Citium
Tyre
Myriandrus
Al Mina (Posidium)
Byblos
Sidon
PHOENICIA
Joppa
Naucratis
DARDANELLES (HELLESPONT)

13. THE ACROPOLIS OF ATHENS FROM MYCENAEAN TIMES TO 470 BC.

Clepsydra
Mycenaean royal palace
Altar to Athena
Pantheon
Propylaea
Old temple
Sanctuary of Nike
The old Parthenon

from Mycenaean period
from 6th century BC.
to 461 BC.

0   40   80 yards

12. ANCIENT CRETE

Achaeans
Minoans

0   20 miles

Phalasarna
Polyrrhenia
Aptara
Sybrita
Ida
Heracleum
Cnossus
Lyctus
Gortyna
Phaestus
Rhytium
Praesus
Itanus

14. ANCIENT GREECE

Greek peoples:

- Ionians
- Dorians
- Aeolians
- Northwest Greeks (North Dorians)
- Arcadians

0 20 40 60 miles

15. CENTRAL GREECE

0 10 20 miles

ILLYRIA

MACEDONIA

Pella

Amphipolis

Philippi

Abdera

THRACE

Thessalonica

Thasos

Samothrace

CHALCIDICE

Pydna

Haliacmon

Mt. Olympus

Heracleum

Olynthus

Potidaea

Mt. Athos

Imbros

CHERSONESUS

Abydos

HELLESPONT

Troy (Ilium)

THRACIAN SEA

Lemnos

Tenedos

Peneus

Vale of Tempe

Europus

Ossa

Larisa

EPIRUS

Dodona

Pelion

THESSALY

Pharsalus

Pindus

Lesbos

Mytilene

Ambracia

Actium

Leucas

Achelous

Lamia

Mt. Oeta

Thermopylae

Peparethos

Scyros

AEGEAN SEA

Phocaea

ACARNANIA

AETOLIA

Parnassus

LOCRIS

LOCRIS

Euboea

Chalcis

Eretria

Chios

Ithaca

Naupactus

Delphi

PHOCIS

BOEOTIA

Tanagra

Cephallenia

GULF OF CORINTH

Leuctra

Thebes

Marathon

Carystus

ACHAEA

Megara

ATTICA

Andros

Samos

Elis

Clitor

Corinth

Athens

Epidaurus

CAPE SUNIUM

Ceos

Tenos

Icaria

Zacynthus

ELIS

Mycenae

ARCADIA

Tiryns

ARGOLIS

Calauria

Cythnos

Cyclades

Syros

Delos

Myconos

Patmos

Olympia

Alpheus

PELOPONNESUS

Hydra

Seriphos

Paros

Naxos

IONIAN SEA

MESSENIA

Taygetus

Sparta

Vaphio

Siphnos

Sicinos

Ios

Amorgos

Sphacteria

Pylus

LACONIA

Melos

Thera

Cythera

SEA OF CRETE

Heracleum (Candia)

Crete

Cnossus

Phaestus

Mt. Parnassus

Orchomenus

Euboea

Aegitium

Delphi

Chaeronea

COPAIS

Chalcis

Polis

PHOCIS

Coronea

BOEOTIA

Aulis

Eretria

Aegium

GULF OF CORINTH

Mt. Helicon

Thebes

Tanagra

ACHAEA

Ascra

Thespiae

Leuctra

Plataea

Decelea

Marathon

Aegira

Sicyon

Megara

Eleusis

ATTICA

Carystus

Andros

Clitor

Stymphalus

Corinth

Salamis

Athens

Piraeus

Nemea

ARGOLIS

Salamis

Mt. Hymettus

Prasiae

ARCADIA

Mycenae

Midea (Dendra)

Aegina

GULF OF SAROS

Mantinea

Argos

Tiryns

Lerna

Asine

Epidaurus

Aegina

CAPE SUNIUM

Ceos

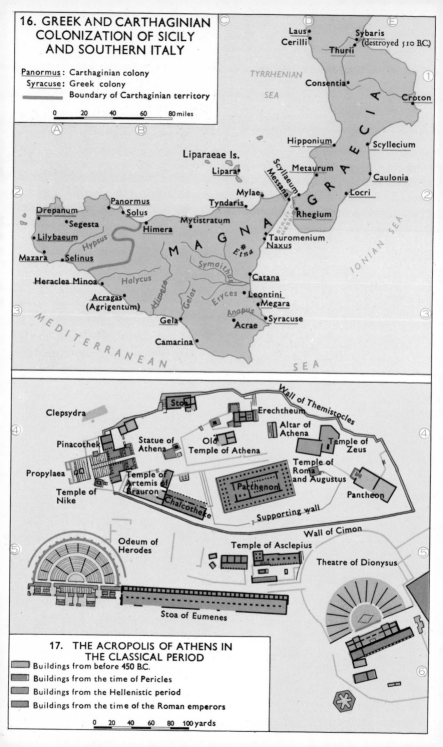

16. GREEK AND CARTHAGINIAN COLONIZATION OF SICILY AND SOUTHERN ITALY

<u>Panormus</u>: Carthaginian colony
<u>Syracuse</u>: Greek colony
Boundary of Carthaginian territory

0   20   40   60   80 miles

TYRRHENIAN
SEA

Laus
Cerilli
Thurii
Sybaris
(destroyed 510 B.C.)
Consentia
Croton
Hipponium
Scyllecium
Metaurum
Caulonia
Scyllaeum
Messana
Mylae
Locri
Tyndaris
Rhegium
Liparaeae Is.
Lipara
Drepanum
Panormus
Solus
Segesta
Himera
Mytistratum
Lilybaeum
Hypsus
MAGNA
Etna
Taurominium
Naxus
Mazara
Selinus
Halycus
Symaithus
Heraclea Minoa
Acragas
(Agrigentum)
Himera
Eryces
Catana
Gelas
Leontini
Gela
Anapus
Megara
Acrae
Syracuse
Camarina

GRAECIA

STRAITS of MESSINA

IONIAN
SEA

MEDITERRANEAN   SEA

17.   THE ACROPOLIS OF ATHENS IN THE CLASSICAL PERIOD

Clepsydra
Stoa
Wall of Themistocles
Erechtheum
Altar of Athena
Pinacothek
Statue of Athena
Old Temple of Athena
Temple of Zeus
Propylaea
Temple of Artemis of Brauron
Temple of Roma and Augustus
Temple of Nike
Chalcotheke
Parthenon
Pantheon
Supporting wall
Wall of Cimon
Odeum of Herodes
Temple of Asclepius
Theatre of Dionysus
Stoa of Eumenes

Buildings from before 450 B.C.
Buildings from the time of Pericles
Buildings from the Hellenistic period
Buildings from the time of the Roman emperors

0   20   40   60   80   100 yards

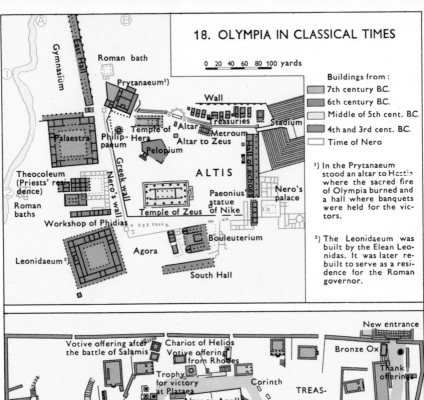

18. OLYMPIA IN CLASSICAL TIMES

0 20 40 60 80 100 yards

Buildings from:

- 7th century B.C.
- 6th century B.C.
- Middle of 5th cent. B.C.
- 4th and 3rd cent. B.C.
- Time of Nero

Gymnasium

East Hall

Roman bath

Prytanaeum[1])

Palaestra

Philip-paeum

Temple of Hera

Pelopium

Wall

Treasuries

Altar

Metroum

Altar to Zeus

Stadium

Theocoleum (Priests' residence)

Roman baths

Workshop of Phidias

Leonidaeum[2])

Temple of Zeus

Agora

Paeonius statue of Nike

South Hall

Bouleuterium

ALTIS

Hall of echoes

Nero's palace

Greek wall

Nero's wall

[1]) In the Prytanaeum stood an altar to Hestia where the sacred fire of Olympia burned and a hall where banquets were held for the victors.

[2]) The Leonidaeum was built by the Elean Leonidas. It was later rebuilt to serve as a residence for the Roman governor.

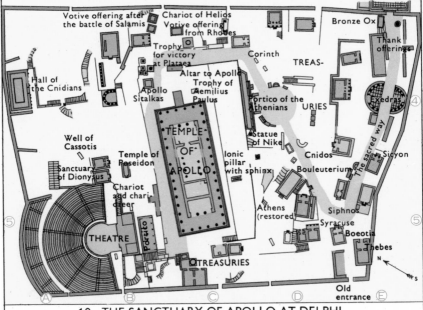

Votive offering after the battle of Salamis

Chariot of Helios

Votive offering from Rhodes

New entrance

Bronze Ox

Thank offerings

Trophy for victory at Plataea

Corinth

TREAS-

Hall of the Cnidians

Apollo Sitalkas

Altar to Apollo

Trophy of Aemilius Paulus

Portico of the Athenians

URIES

Exedra

Well of Cassotis

Temple of Poseidon

TEMPLE OF APOLLO

Statue of Nike

Cnidos

Sicyon

The sacred way

Sanctuary of Dionysus

Chariot and charioteer

Ionic pillar with sphinx

Bouleuterium

Portico

Athens (restored)

Siphnos

THEATRE

Syracuse

Boeotia

Thebes

TREASURIES

Old entrance

19. THE SANCTUARY OF APOLLO AT DELPHI

- Buildings and monuments from before 525 B.C.
- Buildings and monuments from 525-448 B.C.
- Buildings and monuments from 423-321 B.C.
- Buildings and monuments from the period after 321 B.C.

THE TEMPLE OF APOLLO

Destroyed by fire in 548 B.C. Rebuilt magnificently from c. 515 B.C. by the Alcmaeonids. Destroyed by an earthquake in 373 B.C. Rebuilt once more 370-330 B.C.

0 10 20 30 40 50 yards

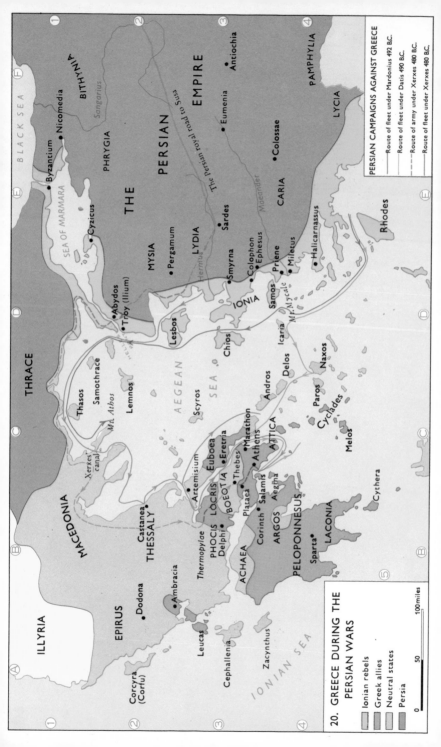

BLACK SEA

THRACE

ILLYRIA

EPIRUS

MACEDONIA

THESSALY

• Dodona
• Ambracia

Leucas

Cephallenia

Zacynthus

Corcyra
(Corfu)

IONIAN SEA

Mt. Athos

Xerxes canal

Thasos

Samothrace

Lemnos

Scyros

AEGEAN SEA

Lesbos

Chios

Icaria

Samos

Mt. Mycale

Naxos

Andros

Delos

Paros

Cyclades

Melos

Cythera

Artemisium

Thermopylae

PHOCIS
Delphi

LOCRIS

Euboea
Eretria

BOEOTIA
Thebes
Plataea

Castanea

Marathon

ATTICA

Athens

Salamis

Megara

Aegina

ACHAEA

Corinth

ARGOS

PELOPONNESUS

LACONIA

Sparta •

SEA OF MARMARA

Byzantium •

Cyzicus •

Abydos •
Troy (Ilium) •

IONIA

Smyrna

Colophon
Ephesus

Priene

Miletus

Halicarnassus

• Nicomedia

BITHYNIA

PHRYGIA

Sangarius

THE PERSIAN EMPIRE

MYSIA

• Pergamum

LYDIA

Hermus

Sardes •

The Persian royal road to Susa

Maeander

CARIA

Meander

• Eumenia

• Colossae

• Antiochia

PAMPHYLIA

LYCIA

Rhodes

PERSIAN CAMPAIGNS AGAINST GREECE

Route of fleet under Mardonius 492 B.C.

Route of fleet under Datis 490 B.C.

Route of army under Xerxes 480 B.C.

Route of fleet under Xerxes 480 B.C.

20. GREECE DURING THE PERSIAN WARS

Ionian rebels

Greek allies

Neutral states

Persia

0   50   100 miles

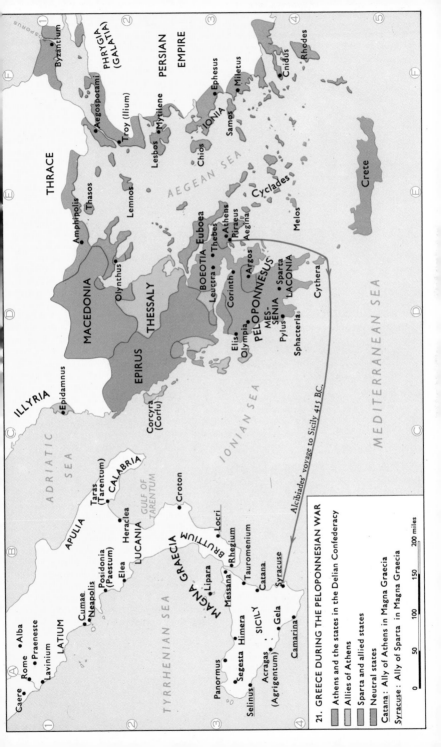

21. GREECE DURING THE PELOPONNESIAN WAR

Athens and the states in the Delian Confederacy

Allies of Athens

Sparta and allied states

Neutral states

Catana: Ally of Athens in Magna Graecia

Syracuse: Ally of Sparta in Magna Graecia

0   50   100   150   200 miles

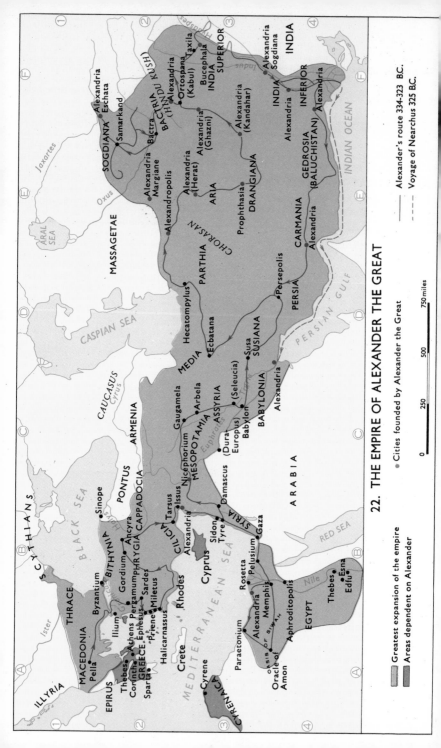

22. THE EMPIRE OF ALEXANDER THE GREAT

- Greatest expansion of the empire
- Areas dependent on Alexander
- Cities founded by Alexander the Great
- —— Alexander's route 334-323 B.C.
- - - - Voyage of Nearchus 325 B.C.

0   250   500   750 miles

ILLYRIA
MACEDONIA
Pella
EPIRUS
THRACE
Byzantium
BITHYNIA
PONTUS
Sinope
SCYTHIANS
BLACK SEA
Ister
Thebes
Corinth
Athens
GREECE
Sparta
Ilium
Pergamum
Ephesus
Sardes
PHRYGIA
Ancyra
Gordium
CAPPADOCIA
Priene
Miletus
Halicarnassus
Crete
Rhodes
Cyprus
CILICIA
Tarsus
Issus
Nicephorium
ARMENIA
CAUCASUS
Cyrus
CASPIAN SEA
ARAL SEA
Jaxartes
Oxus
MASSAGETAE
SOGDIANA
Samarkand
Alexandria Eschata
BACTRIA (HINDU KUSH)
Bactra
Alexandria
Oreospana (Kabul)
Taxila
Alexandria
Bucephala
INDIA SUPERIOR
Hydaspes
Indus
INDIA
Alexandria Sogdiana
INDIA INFERIOR
Alexandria
INDIA
Alexandria (Ghazni)
Alexandria (Kandahar)
Alexandria (Herat)
ARIA
DRANGIANA
Prophthasia
CHORASAN
PARTHIA
Alexandria Margiane
Alexandropolis
Hecatompylus
MEDIA
Ecbatana
Gaugamela
Arbela
(Seleucia)
(Dura-Europus)
Babylon
MESOPOTAMIA
ASSYRIA
Euphrates
Tigris
Damascus
SYRIA
Sidon
Tyre
Gaza
Alexandria
Pelusium
Rosetta
Alexandria
Memphis
EGYPT
Oasis of Siwah
Oracle of Amon
Aphroditopolis
Nile
Thebes
Esna
Edfu
RED SEA
ARABIA
Susa
SUSIANA
Alexandria
BABYLONIA
PERSIA
Persepolis
CARMANIA
Alexandria
GEDROSIA (BALUCHISTAN)
Alexandria
PERSIAN GULF
INDIAN OCEAN
MEDITERRANEAN SEA
Paraetonium
Cyrene
CYRENAICA

23. ITALY BEFORE THE FIRST PUNIC WAR 264 B.C.

- Etruscans
- Greek colonies
- Carthaginian dominions
- Italians
- Other peoples
- Gallic territory
- Southern and northern boundaries of Roman territory 264 B.C.
- Important Roman roads and roads built after 264 B.C.

0   50   100   150 miles

Map 23 labels:

GALLIA TRANSPADANA · Mediolanum · Verona · VENETIA · Patavium · Vercellae · Augusta Taurinorum · Mantua · Cremona · Pola · Placentia · LIGURIA · Via Aemilia · Mutina · Bononia · Padus · GALLIA CISPADANA · Genua · Via Aemilia Scauri · Ravenna · Ariminum · Nicaea · Pisa · Rubico · Florentia · Sena · Ancona · UMBRIA · Arretium · Via Aurelia · Perusia · Camerinum · PICENUM · Ilva · Via Flaminia · Asculum · CORSICA · Vulci · Tarquinii · Veii · SABINA · Via Salaria · AEQUI · Via Valeria · Corfinium · Aleria · Caere · Fidenae · Ostia · Rome · Praeneste · LATIUM · VOLSCI · SAMNIUM · APULIA · Cannae · Terracina · Capua · Beneventum · Neapolis · Vesuvius · Via Appia · Brundisium · Pithecussa · Pompeii · Puteoli · Herculaneum · Paestum · Tarentum · CALABRIA · CAMPANIA · LUCANIA · Heraclea · SARDINIA · Sybaris · Neapolis · Croton · Carales · BRUTTIUM · TYRRHENIAN SEA · Liparaeae Is. · IONIAN SEA · Aegates Is. · Panormus · Messana · Rhegium · Segesta · Lilybaeum · SICILY · Catana (Catania) · Etna · AFRICA · Utica · Agrigentum (Acragas) · Gela · Syracuse · Carthage

24. THE RETREAT OF THE TEN THOUSAND 401-399 B.C.

Route followed by the Greeks, first under the leadership of Cyrus, later under Xenophon

0   100   200 miles

Map 24 labels:

Byzantium (399 BC) · Sinope · Heraclea · CAUCASUS · Cerasus · Cotyora · Trapezus · PONTUS · Abydos · Pergamum · CAPPADOCIA · ARMENIA (400 BC) · Araxes · LYDIA · Sardes (401 BC) · PHRYGIA · Halys · PERSIAN EMPIRE · MEDIA · Ephesus · Priene · Iconium · Tyana · (KURDISTAN) · Miletus · ASSYRIA · Mespila (Nineveh) · Rhodes · CILICIA · Myriandrus · Tarsus · CYPRUS · Thapsacus · MESOPOTAMIA · Euphrates · MEDITERRANEAN SEA · Sidon · Damascus · Cunaxa (401 BC) · Sittace · Babylon · Jerusalem · ARABIA · BABYLONIA

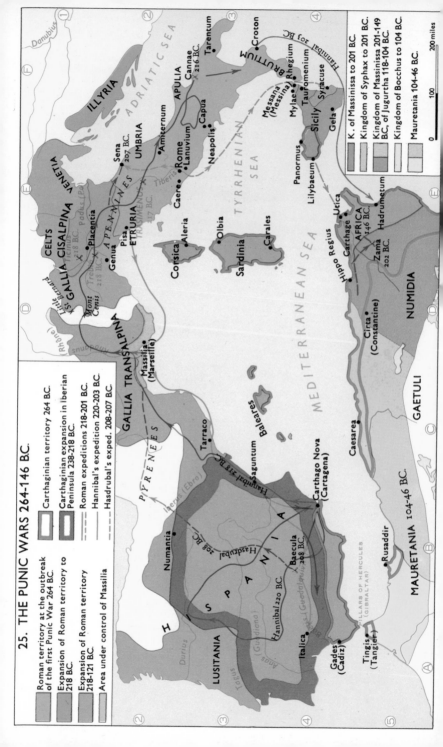

25. THE PUNIC WARS 264-146 B.C.

Roman territory at the outbreak of the first Punic War 264 B.C.

Expansion of Roman territory to 218 B.C.

Expansion of Roman territory 218-121 B.C.

Area under control of Massilia

Carthaginian territory 264 B.C.

Carthaginian expansion in Iberian Peninsula 238-218 B.C.

Roman expeditions 218-201 B.C.

Hannibal's expedition 220-203 B.C.

Hasdrubal's exped. 208-207 B.C.

K. of Massinissa to 201 B.C.

Kingdom of Syphax to 201 B.C.

Kingdom of Massinissa 201-149 B.C. of Jugurtha 118-104 B.C.

Kingdom of Bocchus to 104 B.C.

Mauretania 104-46 B.C.

0   100   200 miles

Place names and labels

Danubius

ILLYRIA

ADRIATIC SEA

CELTS

GALLIA CISALPINA

VENETIA

Little Bernard
St. Bernard
Mont Cenis
Rhodanus (Rhône)

Placentia
Genua
Pisa
APENNINES

Trebia 218 B.C.
Ticinus 218 B.C.
Padus (Po)

UMBRIA
Sena 207 B.C.
Amiternum
Tiberis
Caere
Rome
Lanuvium
ETRURIA
TRASIMENUS 217 B.C.

APULIA
Tarentum
Cannae 216 B.C.
Capua
Neapolis

Croton
BRUTTIUM
Hannibal 203 B.C.
Rhegium
Messana (Messina)
Mylae 260 B.C.
Tauromenium
Syracuse
Sicily
Gela
Panormus
Lilybaeum

TYRRHENIAN SEA

Corsica
Aleria
Olbia
Sardinia
Carales

MEDITERRANEAN SEA

Utica
Carthage
AFRICA 146 B.C.
Hippo Regius
Zama 202 B.C.
Hadrumetum

Cirta (Constantine)
NUMIDIA

GAETULI

GALLIA TRANSALPINA
Massilia (Marseille)

PYRENEES
Tarraco
Iberus (Ebro)

Saguntum
Hannibal 218 B.C.
Baleares

Carthago Nova (Cartagena)
Hasdrubal 208 B.C.
Baecula 208 B.C.
Caesarea

Numantia
S P A N I A
Hannibal 220 B.C.
Baetis (Guadalquivir)

LUSITANIA
Durius
Tagus
Anas (Guadiana)
Italica

Gades (Cadiz)
PILLARS OF HERCULES (GIBRALTAR)
Tingis (Tangier)
Rusaddir

MAURETANIA 104-46 B.C.

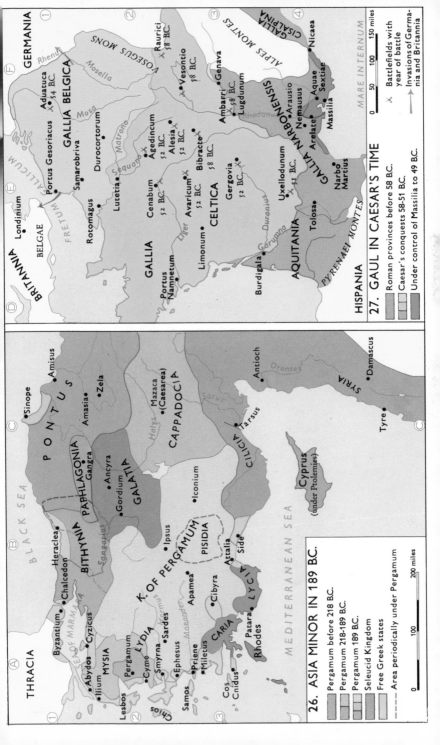

26. ASIA MINOR IN 189 B.C.

THRACIA

BLACK SEA

Byzantium
Chalcedon
Heraclea
Abydos
Ilium

SEA OF MARMARA

Cyzicus
Pergamum
Cyme
Smyrna
Sardes
Ephesus
Priene
Miletus

MYSIA
LYDIA

Lesbos
Chios
Samos
Cos
Cnidus

Maeander

K. OF PERGAMUM

Apamea
Cibyra

CARIA

LYCIA

Patara
Rhodes

MEDITERRANEAN SEA

Sinope
Amisus

PONTUS

PAPHLAGONIA

Amasia
Zela
Gangra
Ancyra
Gordium

GALATIA

Ipsus

PISIDIA

Iconium

Attalia
Side

Mazaca
(Caesarea)

CAPPADOCIA

Halys
Sarus

Tarsus

CILICIA

Cyprus
(under Ptolemies)

Tyre

Antioch

SYRIA

Orontes

Damascus

Sangarius

Pergamum before 218 B.C.
Pergamum 218-189 B.C.
Pergamum 189 B.C.
Seleucid Kingdom
Free Greek states
Area periodically under Pergamum

0   100   200 miles

27. GAUL IN CAESAR'S TIME

GERMANIA

BRITANNIA

Londinium

BELGAE

FRETUM GALLICUM

Portus Gesoriacus

GALLIA BELGICA

Aduatuca ×54 B.C.

Samarobriva

Durocortorum

Rotomagus

Lutetia

Cenabum §52 B.C.

Agedincum §52 B.C.

Alesia §52 B.C.

Avaricum §52 B.C.

Bibracte §58 B.C.

GALLIA

Portus Namnetum

CELTICA

Limonum

Liger

Gergovia §52 B.C.

Uxellodunum

AQUITANIA

Burdigala

Tolosa

Garumna

Duranius

VOSEGUS MONS

Rauraci §58 B.C.

Vesontio §58 B.C.

Lugdunum

Ambarri ×58 B.C.

Genava

Arausio

Nemausus

GALLIA NARBONENSIS

Arelate

Massilia

Narbo Martius

PYRENAEI MONTES

ALPES MONTES

GALLIA CISALPINA

Nicaea

Aquae Sextiae ×

MARE INTERNUM

Rhenus
Germania
Mosella
Mosa
Matrona
Sequana
Rhodanus

HISPANIA

Roman provinces before 58 B.C.
Caesar's conquests 58-51 B.C.
Under control of Massilia to 49 B.C.

× Battlefields with year of battle
→ Invasions of Germania and Britannia

0   50   100   150 miles

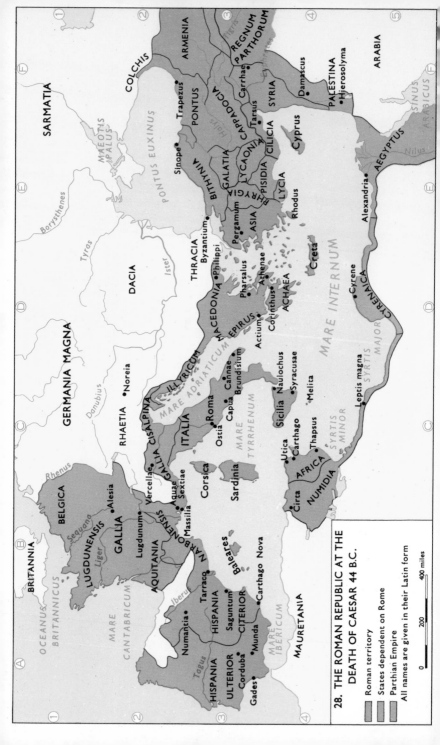

28. THE ROMAN REPUBLIC AT THE DEATH OF CAESAR 44 B.C.

Roman territory
States dependent on Rome
Parthian Empire
All names are given in their Latin form

0   200   400 miles

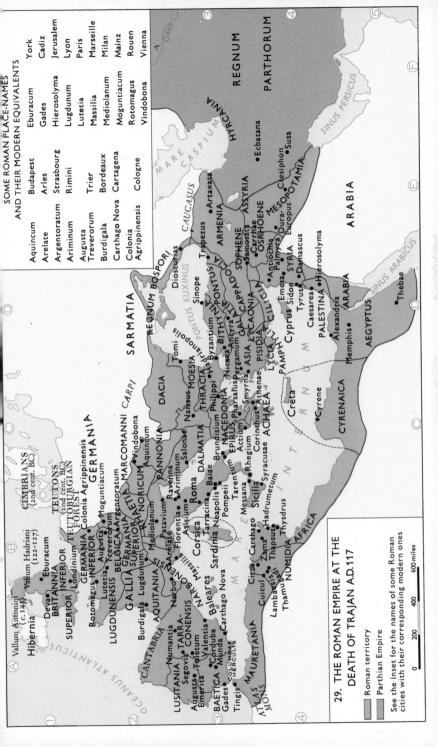

SOME ROMAN PLACE-NAMES AND THEIR MODERN EQUIVALENTS

Aquincum	Budapest
Arelate	Arles
Argentoratum	Strasbourg
Ariminum	Rimini
Augusta Treverorum	Trier
Burdigala	Bordeaux
Carthago Nova	Cartagena
Colonia Agrippinensis	Cologne
Eburacum	York
Gades	Cadiz
Hierosolyma	Jerusalem
Lugdunum	Lyon
Lutetia	Paris
Massilia	Marseille
Mediolanum	Milan
Moguntiacum	Mainz
Rotomagus	Rouen
Vindobona	Vienna

29. THE ROMAN EMPIRE AT THE DEATH OF TRAJAN A.D.117

Roman territory

Parthian Empire

See the inset for the names of some Roman cities with their corresponding modern ones

0   200   400   600 miles

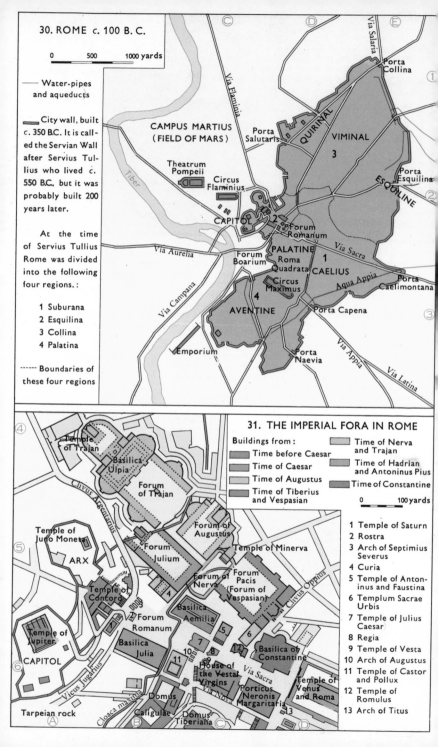

30. ROME c. 100 B.C.

0   500   1000 yards

— Water-pipes and aqueducts

▬ City wall, built c. 350 B.C. It is called the Servian Wall after Servius Tullius who lived c. 550 B.C., but it was probably built 200 years later.

At the time of Servius Tullius Rome was divided into the following four regions. :

1 Suburana
2 Esquilina
3 Collina
4 Palatina

------ Boundaries of these four regions

CAMPUS MARTIUS (FIELD OF MARS)

Via Flaminia
Via Salaria
Porta Collina
Porta Salutaris
QUIRINAL
VIMINAL
3
Porta Esquilina
ESQUILINE
Theatrum Pompeii
Circus Flaminius
Tiber
CAPITOL
2
Forum Romanum
Via Sacra
Via Aurelia
Forum Boarium
PALATINE
Roma Quadrata
1
CAELIUS
Aqua Appia
Porta Caelimontana
Circus Maximus
4
Via Campana
AVENTINE
Porta Capena
Emporium
Porta Naevia
Via Appia
Via Latina

31. THE IMPERIAL FORA IN ROME

Buildings from :

■ Time before Caesar
■ Time of Caesar
■ Time of Augustus
■ Time of Tiberius and Vespasian
■ Time of Nerva and Trajan
■ Time of Hadrian and Antoninus Pius
■ Time of Constantine

0   100 yards

1 Temple of Saturn
2 Rostra
3 Arch of Septimius Severus
4 Curia
5 Temple of Antoninus and Faustina
6 Templum Sacrae Urbis
7 Temple of Julius Caesar
8 Regia
9 Temple of Vesta
10 Arch of Augustus
11 Temple of Castor and Pollux
12 Temple of Romulus
13 Arch of Titus

Temple of Trajan
Basilica Ulpia
Forum of Trajan
Clivus Argentarius
Temple of Juno Moneta
ARX
Forum Julium
Forum of Augustus
Temple of Minerva
Temple of Concord
Forum of Nerva
Forum Pacis (Forum of Vespasiani)
Clivus Oppius
Temple of Jupiter
CAPITOL
Forum Romanum
Basilica Aemilia
Basilica Julia
Basilica of Constantine
Vicus Jugarius
House of the Vestal Virgins
Via Sacra
Temple of Venus and Roma
Tarpeian rock
Cloaca maxima
Domus Caligulae
Domus Tiberiana
Porticus Neronis Margaritaria
Via Nova

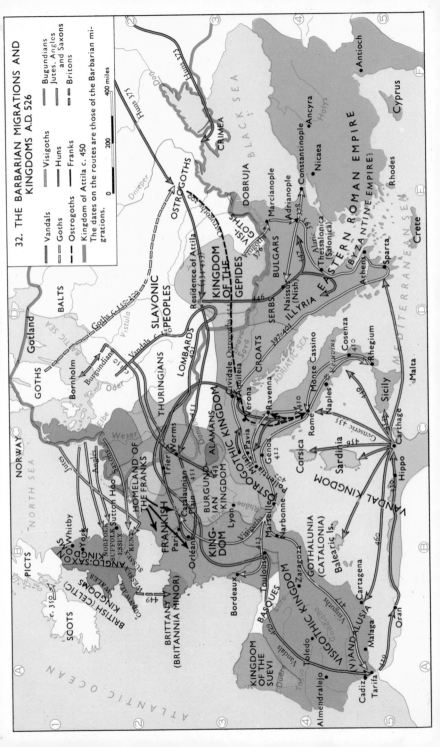

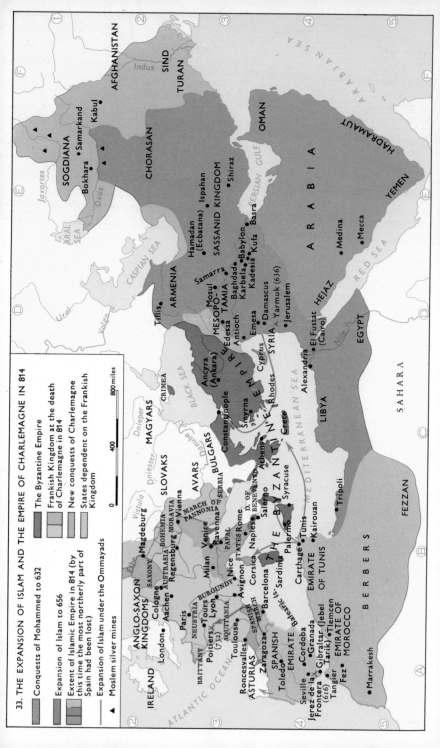

33. THE EXPANSION OF ISLAM AND THE EMPIRE OF CHARLEMAGNE IN 814

Conquests of Mohammed to 632

Expansion of Islam to 656

Extent of Islamic Empire in 814 (by this time the most northerly part of Spain had been lost)

The Byzantine Empire

Frankish Kingdom at the death of Charlemagne in 814

New conquests of Charlemagne

States dependent on the Frankish Kingdom

▲ Moslem silver mines

Expansion of Islam under the Ommayads

0   400   800 miles

34. LOMBARD KINGDOM BEFORE ITS CONQUEST BY CHARLEMAGNE IN 774

- Lombard Kingdom
- Byzantine Empire
- States of the Church (Papal States)

0 100 200 300 miles

FRANKISH
KINGDOM
Trento · Cividale
Milan · Monza
Verona · Venice
Pavia
Genoa · Ravenna
Lucca · PAPAL
Perugia · STATES
SLOVENES
CROATS
Zara
Salona
(Spalato)
Corsica
Spoleto
ADRIATIC SEA
Rome · Monte-
Cassino
Naples · Salerno
Benevento
Taranto
Sardinia
TYRRHENIAN SEA
Palermo · Messina
Sicily · Reggio
Syracuse
Carthage
Tunis

35. EXPANSION OF THE PAPAL STATES 756-817

0 50 miles

Po
Ferrara
Modena
Canossa
Bologna
EXARCHATE
Ravenna
Rimini
Pistoia
Lucca
Florence
Pisa · Vallombrosa
Arno
Urbino
Ancona
TUSCANY
Arezzo
Volterra
Siena
Cortona
Metauro
Populonia
Perugia
Assisi
Trevi
Nursia
Orvieto
Bolsena
PATRIMONIUM
Spoleto
DUCHY OF SPOLETO
Narni
Avezzo
Civita-
vecchia
Rome
Frascati · Subiaco
Palestrina
Ostia · Tusculum
PETRI
Monte
Cassino
Terracina

- Patrimonium Petri (Patrimony of St. Peter) before 756
- Pépin the Short's gift to Papal Chair in 756
- Conquests 757-817
- + Monastery

36. DIVISION OF CHARLEMAGNE'S EMPIRE AT VERDUN IN 843

- Kingdom of Lothair
- Kingdom of Charles the Bald
- Kingdom of Louis the German

0 200 400 miles

IRELAND
MERCIA
Wroxeter
Leicester
Worcester
EAST ANGLIA
NORTH WALES
WEST WALES
WESSEX
KENT
London
Canterbury
SUSSEX
ESSEX
NORTH SEA
Heligoland
HOLSTEIN
Hamburg
WENDLAND
FRIESLAND
Bremen
Utrecht
Osnabrück
Hildesheim
Magdeburg
SAXONY
Elbe
Oder
Warta
Vistula
Münster
Paderborn
Lippespring
Maastricht
Cologne
Fritzlar
Aachen
THURINGIA
HESSE
+ Fulda
BOHEMIA
Bayeux
Rouen
Amiens
Soissons
Rheims
AUSTRASIA
Frankfurt
Ingelheim
Mainz
St.-Denis +
Paris
Verdun
Metz
Trier
Worms
MORAVIA
BRITTANY
Chartres
NEUSTRIA
Troyes
Strasbourg
Regensburg
Angers
Orléans
Fontenoy
Kolmar
ALAMANNIA
Ulm
Zwiefalten
Vienna
Nantes
Tours
Bourges
Besançon
Basel
Zürich
Reichenau
BAVARIA
Salzburg
Kremsmünster
Poitiers
BURGUNDY
Constance
St.-Gall
CARINTHIA
AVAR KINGDOM
Angoulême
Clermont
Geneva
K. OF
Bordeaux
AQUITAINE
Lyon
Vienne
Grenoble
Mt. Cenis
LOMBARDY
Milan
Pavia
Piacenza
Trento
Venice
Turin
Genoa
Parma
Bologna
Ravenna
DALMATIA
K. OF
ASTURIAS
Bayonne
Roncesvalles
GASCONY
SPANISH MARCH
Toulouse
Nîmes
Carcassonne
Narbonne
Avignon
Arles
Marseille
PROVENCE
Nice
Pisa
Florence
TUSCANY
PAPAL
STATES
Ancona
Zaragoza
Barcelona
SPANISH EMIRATE
MEDITERRANEAN SEA
Corsica
Rome
Monte-
Cassino
ITALY
DUCHY OF SPOLETO
D. OF BENEVENTO
Naples
Benevento
Salerno
Brindisi
ADRIATIC SEA

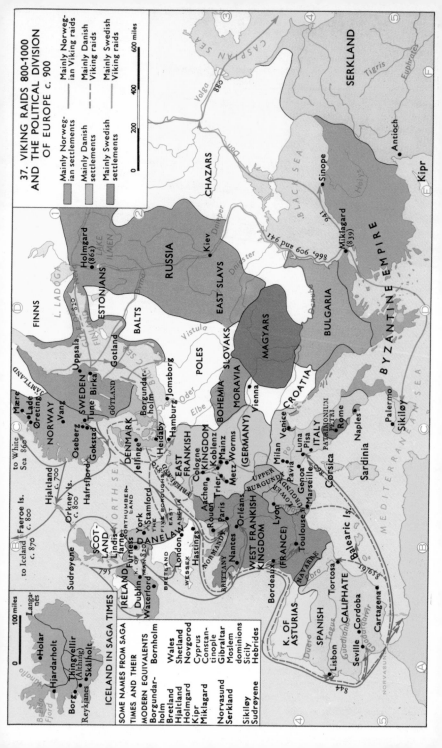

37. VIKING RAIDS 800-1000 AND THE POLITICAL DIVISION OF EUROPE c. 900

▢ Mainly Norweg- ian settlements	Mainly Norweg- ian Viking raids
▢ Mainly Danish settlements	Mainly Danish Viking raids
▢ Mainly Swedish settlements	Mainly Swedish Viking raids

0   200   400   600 miles

ICELAND IN SAGA TIMES

SOME NAMES FROM SAGA TIMES AND THEIR MODERN EQUIVALENTS

Borgundar-holm	Bornholm
Bretland	Wales
Hjaltland	Shetland
Holmgard	Novgorod
Kipr	Cyprus
Miklagard	Constan-tinople
Norvasund	Gibraltar
Serkland	Moslem dominions
Sikiløy	Sicily
Sudrøyene	Hebrides

0   100 miles

38. THE HOLY ROMAN EMPIRE AND THE NORMAN KINGDOM IN SOUTH ITALY

The Kingdom of Germany at the accession of Otto the Great in 936

The Holy Roman Empire in 962, when Otto was crowned emperor

Byzantine territories at end of 10th century

Moslem territory at end of 10th century

→ Magyar raids in 10th century

Norman Kingdom in South Italy at the death of Roger II in 1154

0   100   200   300 miles

K. OF SCOTLAND

Edinburgh

NORTH SEA

IRELAND

Dublin (Danish)

Man

K. OF

Durham

Lancaster

York × Stamford

Cork

Waterford

ENGLAND

Sherwood Forest

Norwich

Bremen

SAXONY

Utrecht

Münster

WALES

Cardiff

Worcester

Oxford

London

Windsor

Canterbury

Exeter

Hastings

Wight

1066

Cologne

Aachen

Gelnhausen

LORRAINE

C. OF FLANDERS

Bouvines

Amiens

C. OF Soissons

Rouen

Bayeux

ATLANTIC OCEAN

D. OF BRITTANY

NORMANDY

Château-Gaillard

Chartres

Paris

Rheims

Trifels FRAN

Worms

Rüdesheim

Weinsberg

Strasbourg

Waiblingen

SWABIA

C. OF MAINE

C. OF ANJOU

Sens

CHAMPAGNE

Orléans

Clairvaux

D. OF BURGUNDY

KINGDOM OF

C. OF POITOU

Poitiers

FRANCE

Cluny

K. OF

Geneva

D. OF AQUITAINE

Clermont

Lyon

Bordeaux

BURGUNDY

Legnano

Milan

Pavia

Piacenza

Roncaglia

Genoa

K. OF LEON

D. OF GASCONY

Toulouse

C. OF

TOULOUSE

Avignon

PROVENCE

Nice

K. OF NAVARRE

K. OF

Burgos

Arles

Carcassonne

Marseille

Oporto

C. OF PORTUGAL

K. OF ARAGON

C. OF CATALONIA (BARCELONA)

Corsica

Zaragoza

Lerida

CASTILE

Madrid

Toledo

Barcelona

Merida

Sardinia

Valencia

Balearic Is.

Cordoba

Seville

Alicante

MEDITERRA

Granada

Cartagena

Cadiz

Tangier

Ceuta

CALIPHATE OF CORDOBA

DOMINIONS OF THE ALMORAVIDES

Oran

Tunis

Duero

Tagus

Guadiana

Guadalquivir

Ebro

Rhine

Maas

Loire

Rhône

Cre

39. EUROPE IN 1100

The Holy Roman Empire
Kingdom of Canute 1028-35
William the Conqueror's invasion of England in 1066
For English possessions in France, see Map 50

0   100   200 miles

NORWAY
Oslo
Uppsala
K. OF
SWEDEN
Dagö
ESTONIA
Ösel
Gotland
. OF
Kalmar
Öland
BALTIC SEA
LITHUANIA
DENMARK
Lund
Bornholm
Memel
OLSTEIN
HOLSTEIN
MECKLEN-BURG
imburg
Lüneburg
PRUSSIA
POMERANIA
RUSSIAN PRINCIPALITIES
Brandenburg
Warta
Vistula
Dnieper
Brunswick
Kyffhäuser
K. OF POLAND
Wartburg
Breslau
isenach
Erfurt
Main
Krakow
Dniester
Bug
Prague
BOHEMIA
Bamberg
ONIA
HOLY
MORAVIA
Dürnstein
Pressburg
Theiss
Prut
CUMANS
(Turks)
Hohenstaufen
BAVARIA
Vienna
Lechfeld
Salzburg
Buda
Pest
ROMAN
KINGDOM OF HUNGARY
TRANSYL-VANIA
Merano
EMPIRE
Brescia
Venice
Sava
Drava
remona
VENICE
CROATIA
Belgrade
Danube
anossa
Bologna
Ravenna
Zara
SERBIA
BLACK SEA
OF
Spalato
BULGARS
sa
Florence
ADRIATIC SEA
Ragusa
ITALY
Maritsa
Spoleto
Adrianople
PAPAL STATES
Rome
Durazzo
Constantinople
Albano
D. OF
Vardar
Thessalonica
Nicaea
Aquino
APULIA
Bari
Naples
Salerno
Brindisi
Amalfi
Taranto
EPIRUS
BYZANTINE EMPIRE
NORMAN
Lesbos
Cotrone
AEGEAN SEA
Ephesus
Messina
Athens
Palermo
C. OF SICILY
KINGDOM
Corinth
Syracuse
Rhodes
79-1389
EAN SEA
Crete

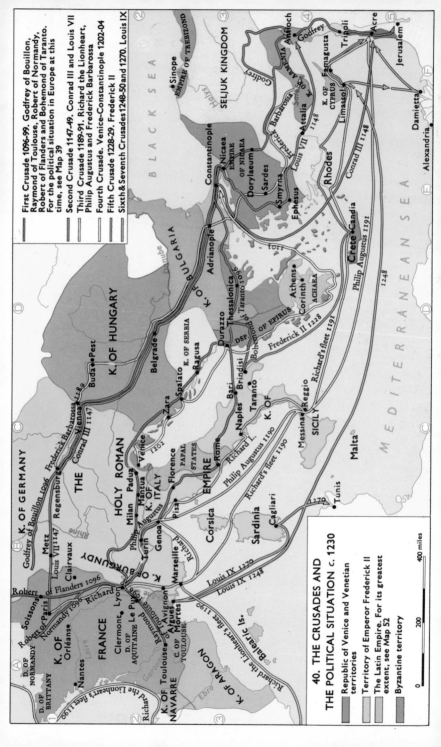

First Crusade 1096-99. Godfrey of Bouillon, Raymond of Toulouse, Robert of Normandy, Robert of Flanders and Bohemond of Taranto. For the political situation in Europe at this time, see Map 39

Second Crusade 1147-49. Conrad III and Louis VII

Third Crusade 1189-91. Richard the Lionheart, Philip Augustus and Frederick Barbarossa

Fourth Crusade. Venice-Constantinople 1202-04

Fifth Crusade 1228-29. Frederick II

Sixth & Seventh Crusades 1248-50 and 1270. Louis IX

40. THE CRUSADES AND
THE POLITICAL SITUATION c. 1230

Republic of Venice and Venetian territories

Territory of Emperor Frederick II

The Latin Empire. For its greatest extent, see Map 52

Byzantine territory

0   200   400 miles

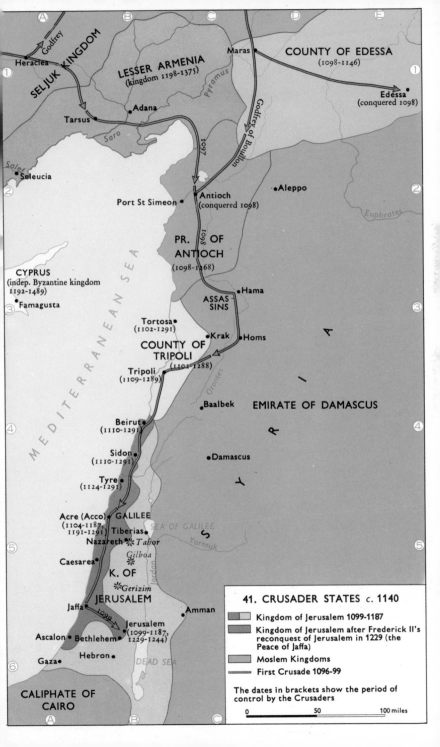

Godfrey

Heraclea

SELJUK KINGDOM

LESSER ARMENIA
(kingdom 1198-1375)

Tarsus

Adana

Seleucia

CYPRUS
(indep. Byzantine kingdom
1192-1489)

Famagusta

Saret

Saro

Pyramus

Maras

COUNTY OF EDESSA
(1098-1146)

Godfrey of Bouillon

Edessa
(conquered 1098)

1097

Port St Simeon

Antioch
(conquered 1098)

Aleppo

Euphrates

PR. OF ANTIOCH
(1098-1268)

1098

ASSAS-
SINS

Hama

Tortosa
(1102-1291)

Krak

Homs

COUNTY OF
TRIPOLI (1102-1288)

Tripoli
(1109-1289)

Orontes

Baalbek

EMIRATE OF DAMASCUS

S   Y   R   I   A

Beirut
(1110-1291)

Sidon
(1110-1291)

Damascus

Tyre
(1124-1291)

Acre (Acco) GALILEE
(1104-1187,
1191-1291)

Tiberias

Nazareth *Tabor

SEA OF GALILEE

Yarmuk

Caesarea

Gilboa

Jordan

K. OF

*Gerizim

JERUSALEM

Jaffa

1099

Amman

Jerusalem
(1099-1187,
1229-1244)

Ascalon Bethlehem

Gaza

Hebron

DEAD SEA

CALIPHATE OF
CAIRO

M E D I T E R R A N E A N   S E A

41. CRUSADER STATES c. 1140

Kingdom of Jerusalem 1099-1187

Kingdom of Jerusalem after Frederick II's
reconquest of Jerusalem in 1229 (the
Peace of Jaffa)

Moslem Kingdoms

First Crusade 1096-99

The dates in brackets show the period of
control by the Crusaders

0   50   100 miles

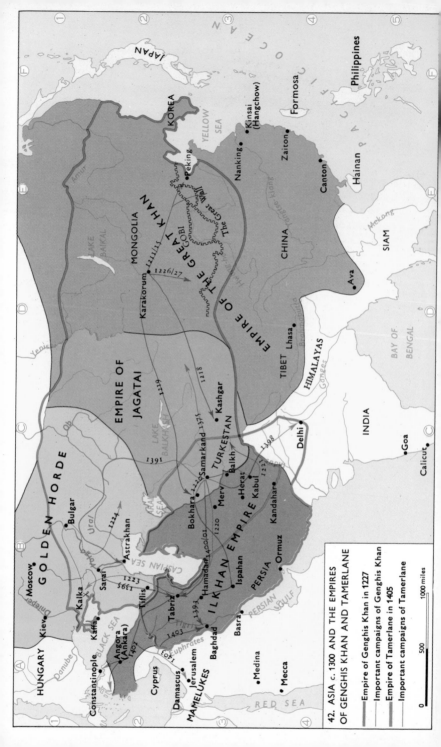

42. ASIA c. 1300 AND THE EMPIRES
OF GENGHIS KHAN AND TAMERLANE

Empire of Genghis Khan in 1227
Important campaigns of Genghis Khan
Empire of Tamerlane in 1405
Important campaigns of Tamerlane

0   500   1000 miles

EMPIRE OF THE GREAT KHAN

EMPIRE OF JAGATAI

GOLDEN HORDE

ILKHAN EMPIRE

MAMELUKES

PERSIA

CHINA

TURKESTAN

MONGOLIA

TIBET

INDIA

SIAM

KOREA

JAPAN

HUNGARY

Philippines

Formosa

Hainan

Cyprus

BAY OF BENGAL

RED SEA

PERSIAN GULF

CASPIAN SEA

BLACK SEA

ARAL SEA

LAKE BAIKAL

LAKE BALKHASH

YELLOW SEA

Moscow
Kiev
Kalka
Bulgar
Astrakhan
Sarai
Tiflis
Constantinople
Angora (Ankara)
Damascus
Jerusalem
Medina
Mecca
Baghdad
Basra
Ispahan
Tabriz
Ormuz
Hamadan
Kandahar
Kabul
Herat
Balkh
Merv
Bokhara
Samarkand
Kashgar
Delhi
Goa
Calicut
Lhasa
Ava
Karakorum
Peking
Nanking
Kinsai (Hangchow)
Zaiton
Canton
Kaffa

The Great Wall
GOBI

Dnieper
Danube
Ural
Ob
Yenisei
Amur
Volga
Don
Euphrates
Tigris
Indus
Ganges
Brahmaputra
Mekong
Yangtse Kiang
Hwang-ho

HIMALAYAS

1211/15
1226/27
1218
1219
1220
1221
1223
1224
1371
1398
1391
1395
1393
1402
1401

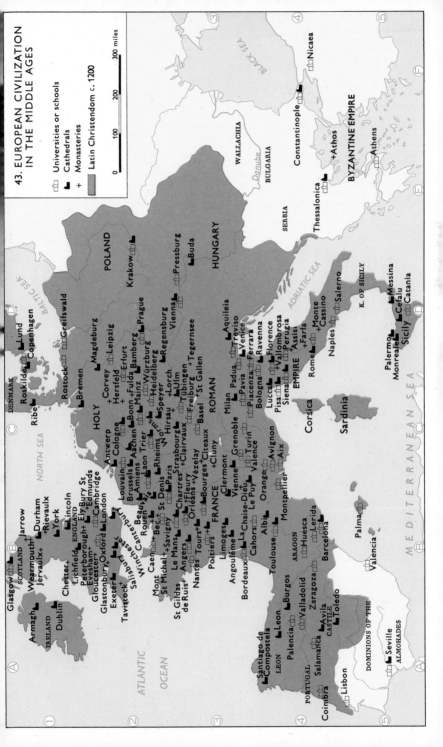

43. EUROPEAN CIVILIZATION IN THE MIDDLE AGES

- ☐ Universities or schools
- ◼ Cathedrals
- + Monasteries
- ▓ Latin Christendom c. 1200

0   100   200   300 miles

BALTIC SEA
NORTH SEA
ATLANTIC OCEAN
MEDITERRANEAN SEA
ADRIATIC SEA
BLACK SEA

IRELAND
Armagh
Dublin

SCOTLAND
Glasgow

Jarrow
Wearmouth+
Jervaulx+
Durham
+Rievaulx
York
Chester
Lichfield
Lincoln
ENGLAND
Peterborough+ Ely +Bury St.
Eynsham+ +Edmunds
Gloucester+ Cambridge
Glastonbury+ Oxford
Exeter London
Tavistock+
Salisbury+
Winchester+
Canterbury

DENMARK
Ribe
Roskilde
Copenhagen
Lund

Rostock
Greifswald
Bremen
Hamburg
POLAND
Magdeburg
Leipzig
Corvey+
Hersfeld+
Erfurt
Prague
Krakow

Antwerp
Cologne
Louvain
Brussels
Aachen
Bonn +Fulda Bamberg
Trier Mainz
Laon Würzburg
Rheims+ Speyer +Lorch
Paris Hirsau+ Regensburg
Strasbourg +Freiburg +Tegernsee
Chartres +Clairvaux Tübingen Vienna
St Denis +Fleury Basel +St Gallen
Orléans +Vézelay HOLY ROMAN EMPIRE
Bourges +Cîteaux
+Cluny
Heidelberg
Ulm

HUNGARY
Pressburg
Buda

WALLACHIA
Danube
BULGARIA
SERBIA

Bec+
Caen
Mont St Michel+
St Gildas
de Ruis+
Angers
Nantes
Tours+
Poitiers
FRANCE
Limoges
Angoulême
Bordeaux
La Chaise-Dieu+
Cahors
Albi
Toulouse
Clermont
Le Puy
Vienne
Valence
Grenoble
Orange
Avignon
Aix
Turin
Montpellier

Milan
Pavia Padua
Piacenza Ferrara
Bologna
Lucca Ravenna
Pisa Florence
Siena +Vallombrosa
Perugia
Assisi +Farfa
Rome
Monte
Cassino+
Naples
Salerno

Aquileia
Treviso
Venice

Corsica
Sardinia

K. OF SICILY
Palermo
Monreale
Cefalu
Messina
Catania
Sicily

LEON
Santiago de
Compostela
Leon
Palencia
Salamanca
PORTUGAL
Coimbra
Lisbon

Burgos
Valladolid
Avila
CASTILE
Toledo

ARAGON
Huesca
Lerida
Zaragoza
Barcelona
Palma
Valencia

DOMINIONS OF THE
ALMOHADES
Seville

BYZANTINE EMPIRE
Constantinople
+Athos
Thessalonica
Athens
Nicaea

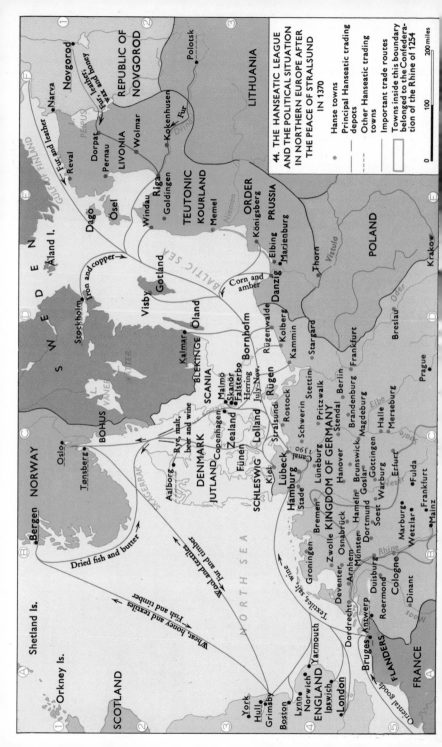

44. THE HANSEATIC LEAGUE AND THE POLITICAL SITUATION IN NORTHERN EUROPE AFTER THE PEACE OF STRALSUND IN 1370

- ● Hanse towns
- ● Principal Hanseatic trading depots
- ● Other Hanseatic trading towns
- —— Important trade routes
- ---- Towns inside this boundary belonged to the Confederation of the Rhine of 1254

0   100   200 miles

ORKNEY Is.

SHETLAND Is.

SCOTLAND

York
Hull
Grimsby
Lynn
Boston
Norwich
Yarmouth
Ipswich
London

ENGLAND

NORTH SEA

Wheat, honey and textiles
Fish and timber
Wool and textiles
Fur and timber
Textiles, salt, wine
Oriental goods

NORWAY

Bergen
Tønsberg
Oslo

Dried fish and butter

BOHUS
SKAGERRAK

SWEDEN

Stockholm
Iron and copper →

L. VÄNERN
L. VÄTTERN

Butter →

Kalmar
Öland
Gotland
Visby

ÅLAND I.

GULF OF FINLAND

Fur and leather →

Reval
Narva
Novgorod

Fur, leather; wax and honey

REPUBLIC OF NOVGOROD

Polotsk

Dago
Ösel
Windau
Goldingen
Riga
Wolmar
Pernau
Dorpat
Fur →
Kokenhusen
Fur →

LIVONIA

PEIPUS

LITHUANIA

TEUTONIC ORDER
KOURLAND
Memel
Königsberg
Niemen

PRUSSIA
Elbing
Marienburg
Thorn

BALTIC SEA

Corn and amber

Danzig
Rügenwalde
Kolberg
Kammin
Stargard
Vistula

POLAND

Krakow
Breslau
Oder
Frankfurt
Prague

DENMARK
JUTLAND
Aalborg
Rye, malt, beer and wine
Copenhagen
Zealand
Fünen
Malmö
Skanör
Falsterbo
Herring →
Jul.-Nov.
SCANIA
BLEKINGE
Bornholm

Lolland
SCHLESWIG
Kiel

Stralsund
Rügen
Rostock
Schwerin
Pritzwalk
Stettin

KINGDOM OF GERMANY

Lübeck
Hamburg
Stade
Bremen
Lüneburg
Hanover
Brunswick
Goslar
Göttingen
Hameln
Brandenburg
Stendal
Berlin
Magdeburg
Halle
Merseburg
Erfurt
Elbe
Weser
Canal 1390

Groningen
Zwolle
Deventer
Arnhem
Osnabrück
Münster
Dortmund
Soest
Warburg
Fulda
Marburg
Wetzlar
Frankfurt
Mainz

Dordrecht
Antwerp
Bruges
Roermond
Duisburg
Cologne
Dinant
Rhine
Maas

FLANDERS

FRANCE

45. RENAISSANCE ITALY

Boundaries after the Peace of Lodi, 1454

0   50   100 miles

46. ACTIVITIES OF THE MEDICI AND FUGGERS IN WESTERN AND CENTRAL EUROPE c. 1500

- ● The Medici city (Florence) and branches
- ● The Fugger city (Augsburg) and branches
- ⚒ Fugger mines and iron-works
- —— Most important commercial routes of the Medici
- —— Most important commercial routes of the Fuggers

Map 45 labels:

Rhône
LAKE MAGGIORE
DUCHY OF SAVOY
Turin
Casale
Asti
MONT-
FERRAT
Como
Milan
Pavia
Lodi
Bicocca
Crema
DUCHY OF MILAN
Piacenza
Parma
Reggio
Berceto
(to Savoy)
REP. OF GENOA
Genoa
Corsica (Genoa)
Bergamo
Brescia
REP.
LAKE GARDA
Trent
Castelfranco
Feltre
OF VENICE
Verona
Vicenza
Padua
Este
MANTUA
Cremona
Mantua
Gonzaga
Mirandola
Correggio
Modena
DUCHY OF MODENA
DUCHY OF FERRARA
Ferrara
Bologna
Ravenna
Faenza
ROMAGNA
Rimini
Pesaro
LUCCA
Lucca
Pisa
San Miniato
REP. OF
Prato
Fiesole
Vinci
Florence
FLORENCE
Arezzo
Caprese
Anghiari
Urbino
Sinigaglia
Ancona
Siena
REP. OF SIENA
DUCHY OF PIOMBINO
Elba
Grosseto
Chiusi
Pitigliano
Orvieto
Bolsena
UMBRIA
Perugia
Assisi
Spoleto
PAPAL
Fermo
Ascoli
Atri
STATES
Corneto
Rome
Ostia
ABRUZZI
KINGDOM OF NAPLES
(Aragon)
Tivoli
Palestrina
Fossanova
Aquino
Capua
Naples
Pieve di Cadore
Trieste
Pirano
Pola
ADRIATIC SEA
Piave
Venice
TYRRHENIAN SEA
Tiber

Map 46 labels:

ATLANTIC OCEAN
London
Bruges
Antwerp
Cologne
Frankfurt
Leipzig
Erfurt
Krakow
Breslau
Teschen
Nuremberg
Vienna
K. OF FRANCE
Augsburg
Innsbruck
Salzburg
Buda (Ofen)
K. OF HUNGARY
Geneva
Lyon
Milan
Venice
OTTOMAN EMPIRE
Genoa
Pisa
Avignon
Florence
Marseille
Rome
Naples
K. OF SPAIN
Madrid
Barcelona
K. OF PORTUGAL
Lisbon
Almaden
Guadalcanal
Seville
MEDITERRANEAN SEA

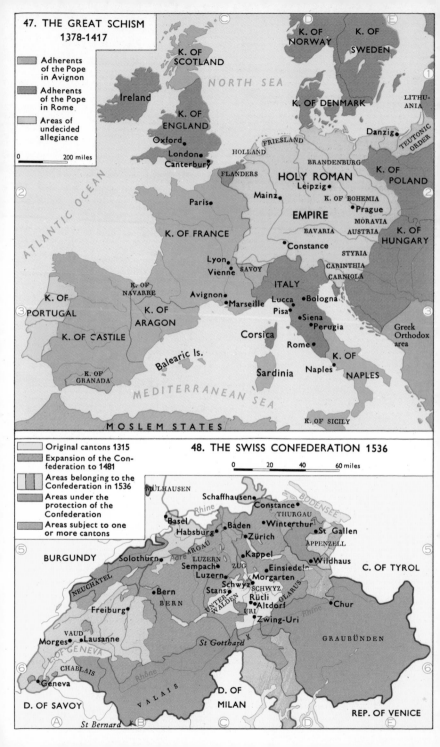

47. THE GREAT SCHISM 1378-1417

Adherents of the Pope in Avignon

Adherents of the Pope in Rome

Areas of undecided allegiance

0   200 miles

NORTH SEA

ATLANTIC OCEAN

K. OF NORWAY

K. OF SWEDEN

K. OF SCOTLAND

Ireland

LITHU-ANIA

K. OF DENMARK

K. OF ENGLAND

Danzig

TEUTONIC ORDER

Oxford

London

Canterbury

FRIESLAND

HOLLAND

FLANDERS

BRANDENBURG

K. OF POLAND

HOLY ROMAN

Leipzig

Mainz

K. OF BOHEMIA

Prague

EMPIRE

MORAVIA

AUSTRIA

K. OF HUNGARY

Paris

K. OF FRANCE

BAVARIA

Constance

STYRIA

CARINTHIA

CARNIOLA

Lyon

Vienne

SAVOY

ITALY

Avignon

Marseille

Lucca

Pisa

Bologna

Siena

Perugia

K. OF NAVARRE

K. OF PORTUGAL

K. OF ARAGON

K. OF CASTILE

Corsica

Rome

Naples

K. OF NAPLES

Greek Orthodox area

Balearic Is.

K. OF GRANADA

Sardinia

MEDITERRANEAN SEA

MOSLEM STATES

K. OF SICILY

48. THE SWISS CONFEDERATION 1536

Original cantons 1315

Expansion of the Confederation to 1481

Areas belonging to the Confederation in 1536

Areas under the protection of the Confederation

Areas subject to one or more cantons

0   20   40   60 miles

MÜLHAUSEN

Rhine

BODENSEE

Schaffhausen

Constance

THURGAU

Basel

Habsburg

Baden

Winterthur

St Gallen

AARGAU

Zürich

APPENZELL

BURGUNDY

Solothurn

Aare

LUZERN

Kappel

Sempach

ZUG

Einsiedeln

Wildhaus

C. OF TYROL

Luzern

Schwyz

Morgarten

SCHWYZ

GLARUS

Chur

Bern

BERN

Stans

UNTERWALDEN

Rütli

URI

Altdorf

Zwing-Uri

NEUCHÂTEL

Freiburg

VAUD

Morges

Lausanne

L. OF GENEVA

St Gotthard

Rhine

GRAUBÜNDEN

CHABLAIS

Geneva

VALAIS

Rhone

D. OF MILAN

REP. OF VENICE

D. OF SAVOY

St Bernard

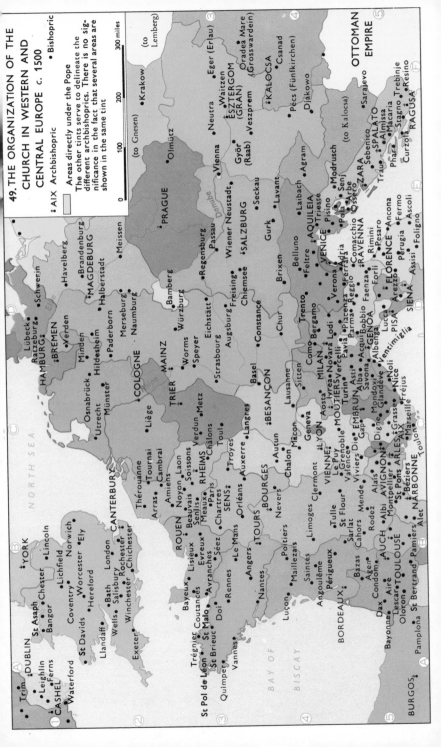

49. THE ORGANIZATION OF THE CHURCH IN WESTERN AND CENTRAL EUROPE c. 1500

‡ AIX Archbishopric ● Bishopric

Areas directly under the Pope

The other tints serve to delineate the different archbishoprics. There is no significance in the fact that several areas are shown in the same tint

0 100 200 300 miles

OTTOMAN EMPIRE

NORTH SEA

BAY OF BISCAY

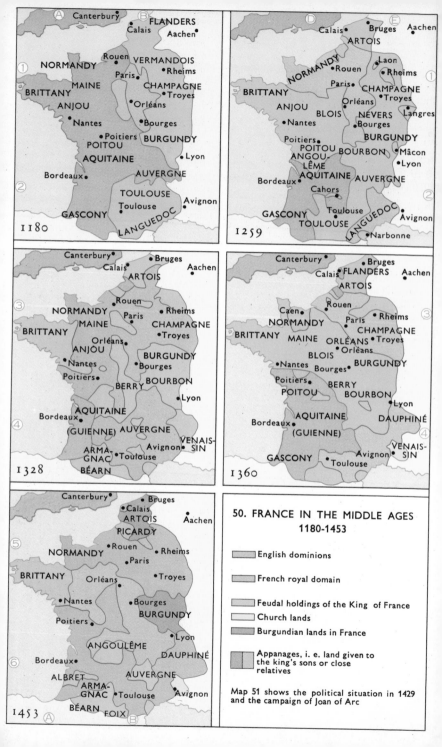

50. FRANCE IN THE MIDDLE AGES 1180-1453

English dominions

French royal domain

Feudal holdings of the King of France

Church lands

Burgundian lands in France

Appanages, i. e. land given to the king's sons or close relatives

Map 51 shows the political situation in 1429 and the campaign of Joan of Arc

51. ENGLAND AND FRANCE IN 1429

- English possessions
- Lands of the French crown
- Feudal holdings of the French crown
- Church lands
- Burgundian lands
- Joan of Arc's campaign

0   50   100   150   200 miles

ULSTER

IRELAND

Dublin

K. OF SCOTLAND

NORTHUMBERLAND

Carlisle
CUMBERLAND
Richmond
Man
Lancaster YORKSHIRE
LANCASTER
York
Towton
Wakefield
Conway
K. OF ENGLAND
LINCOLN
Shrewsbury
NOTTINGHAM
WALES
Nottingham
LEICESTER
Bosworth NORFOLK
WARWICK
Kenilworth Ely
WORCESTER Warwick
HEREFORD BED- Cambridge
GLOU- FORD SUFFOLK
Gloucester CESTER HERTFORD
Berkeley Oxford ESSEX
Bristol Windsor London
Bath SOMERSET WILT- SURREY KENT
SHIRE Canterbury
CORNWALL DEVON HAMPSHIRE
DORSET SUSSEX

NORTH SEA

ENGLISH CHANNEL

HOLLAND

ZEELAND
Blankenberghe Sluys
Bruges Ghent
Calais Ypres FLANDERS BRABANT
ARTOIS Lille Brussels LIM-
Agincourt Arras Liège BURG
Crécy HAINAULT Namur Limburg
PICARDY
Cherbourg Amiens
Harfleur Péronne LUXEMBOURG
Caen Rouen
NORMANDY Beauvais VALOIS Laon RETHEL
Compiègne Soissons
ILE-DE-FRANCE Rheims
St Denis Châlons
BRITTANY Paris CHAMPAGNE
MAINE Chartres Brétigny Nancy
Patay Montereau Domrémy
ORLÉANS Sens Troyes LORRAINE
ANJOU Blois Orléans Auxerre
Nantes Plessis Tours
Chinon Amboise Dijon
Bourges NEVERS Besançon
BERRY Nevers FRANCHE-
POITOU BOURBON BURGUNDY COMTÉ
Poitiers
La Rochelle Geneva
Limoges DUCHY OF SAVOY
BAY OF BISCAY Clermont Lyon
Vienne
Blaye AUVERGNE Le Puy DAUPHINÉ
AQUITAINE
(GUIENNE) Cahors
Bordeaux Rodez VENAISSIN
GASCONY Albi Avignon
Bayonne ARMAGNAC Castres LANGUEDOC PROVENCE
BÉARN Toulouse Marseille
K. OF Narbonne Toulon
NAVARRE
K. OF K. OF ARAGON MEDITERRANEAN SEA
CASTILE

Cologne

Rhine

Maas

Meuse

Seine

Loire

Rhône

Dordogne

Ebro

COLOGNE

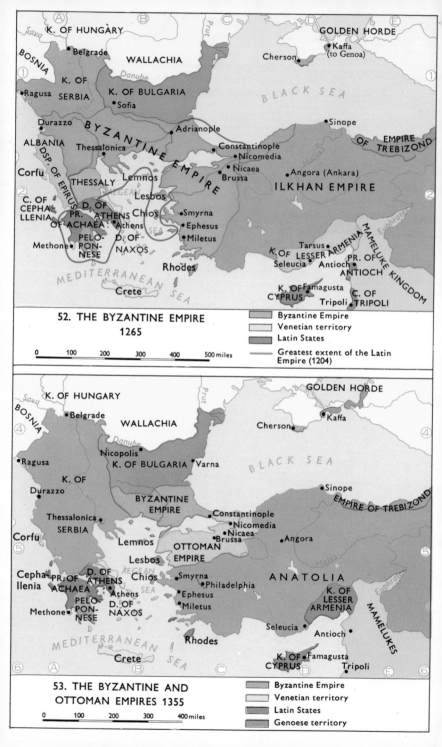

52. THE BYZANTINE EMPIRE 1265

K. OF HUNGARY
BOSNIA
Belgrade
WALLACHIA
GOLDEN HORDE
Kaffa (to Genoa)
Cherson
Ragusa
K. OF SERBIA
K. OF BULGARIA
Sofia
BLACK SEA
Durazzo
ALBANIA
DSP. OF EPIRUS
BYZANTINE EMPIRE
Adrianople
Sinope
EMPIRE OF TREBIZOND
Corfu
Thessalonica
Constantinople
Nicomedia
Nicaea
Brussa
C. OF CEPHALLENIA
THESSALY
Lemnos
Angora (Ankara)
ILKHAN EMPIRE
D. OF ATHENS
PR. OF ACHAEA
Lesbos
Chios
Smyrna
Athens
Ephesus
D. OF NAXOS
Miletus
Methone
PELO-PONNESE
Rhodes
K. OF LESSER ARMENIA
Tarsus
Seleucia
Antioch
PR. OF ANTIOCH
MAMELUKE KINGDOM
Crete
MEDITERRANEAN SEA
K. OF CYPRUS
Famagusta
Tripoli
C. OF TRIPOLI

	Byzantine Empire
	Venetian territory
	Latin States
—	Greatest extent of the Latin Empire (1204)

0   100   200   300   400   500 miles

53. THE BYZANTINE AND OTTOMAN EMPIRES 1355

K. OF HUNGARY
BOSNIA
Belgrade
WALLACHIA
GOLDEN HORDE
Kaffa
Cherson
Ragusa
Nicopolis
K. OF BULGARIA
Varna
BLACK SEA
Durazzo
K. OF SERBIA
BYZANTINE EMPIRE
Sinope
EMPIRE OF TREBIZOND
Thessalonica
Constantinople
Nicomedia
Nicaea
Brussa
Angora
Corfu
Lemnos
OTTOMAN EMPIRE
Halys
Cephalonia
Lesbos
Chios
ANATOLIA
PR. OF ACHAEA
D. OF ATHENS
Smyrna
Philadelphia
Athens
Ephesus
D. OF NAXOS
Miletus
K. OF LESSER ARMENIA
Methone
PELO-PONNESE
Rhodes
Seleucia
Antioch
MAMELUKES
Crete
MEDITERRANEAN SEA
K. OF CYPRUS
Famagusta
Tripoli

	Byzantine Empire
	Venetian territory
	Latin States
	Genoese territory

0   100   200   300   400 miles

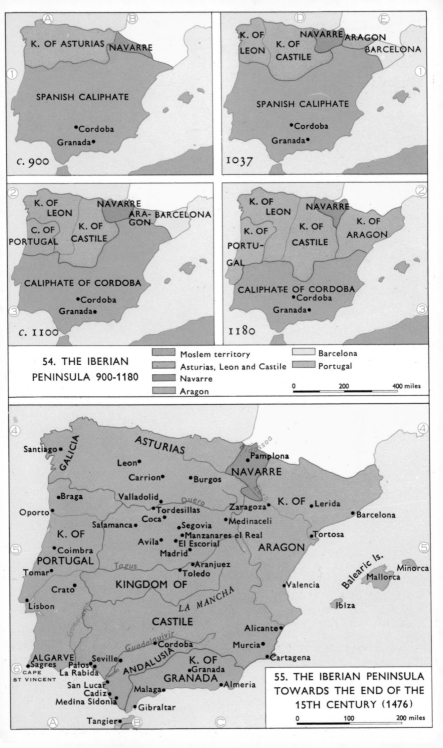

54. THE IBERIAN PENINSULA 900-1180

Moslem territory
Asturias, Leon and Castile
Navarre
Aragon
Barcelona
Portugal

0   200   400 miles

c. 900

K. OF ASTURIAS   NAVARRE

SPANISH CALIPHATE

•Cordoba
Granada•

1037

K. OF LEON   NAVARRE   ARAGON
K. OF CASTILE   BARCELONA

SPANISH CALIPHATE

•Cordoba
Granada•

c. 1100

K. OF LEON   NAVARRE
C. OF PORTUGAL   K. OF CASTILE   ARA-BARCELONA
GON

CALIPHATE OF CORDOBA

•Cordoba
Granada•

1180

K. OF LEON   NAVARRE
K. OF PORTUGAL   K. OF CASTILE   K. OF ARAGON

CALIPHATE OF CORDOBA

•Cordoba
Granada•

55. THE IBERIAN PENINSULA TOWARDS THE END OF THE 15TH CENTURY (1476)

0   100   200 miles

Santiago•
GALICIA
ASTURIAS
Leon•
NAVARRE
Pamplona•
Carrion•
•Burgos
Braga•
Valladolid•
Duero
Zaragoza•
K. OF
Lerida•
Oporto•
Tordesillas•
•Barcelona
Salamanca• Coca•
Medinaceli•
•Segovia
ARAGON
Tortosa•
K. OF
Avila• •Manzanares el Real
•El Escorial
•Coimbra
Madrid•
PORTUGAL
Tagus
•Aranjuez
Tomar•
•Toledo
Valencia•
Balearic Is.
Minorca
Crato•
KINGDOM OF
Mallorca
Lisbon•
LA MANCHA
Ibiza
CASTILE
Alicante•
Murcia•
•Cordoba
ALGARVE
•Seville
Cartagena•
Sagres
Palos•
ANDALUSIA
K. OF
CAPE
La Rabida•
•Granada
ST VINCENT
San Lucar•
GRANADA
Malaga•
•Almeria
Cadiz•
Medina Sidonia•
•Gibraltar
Tangier•

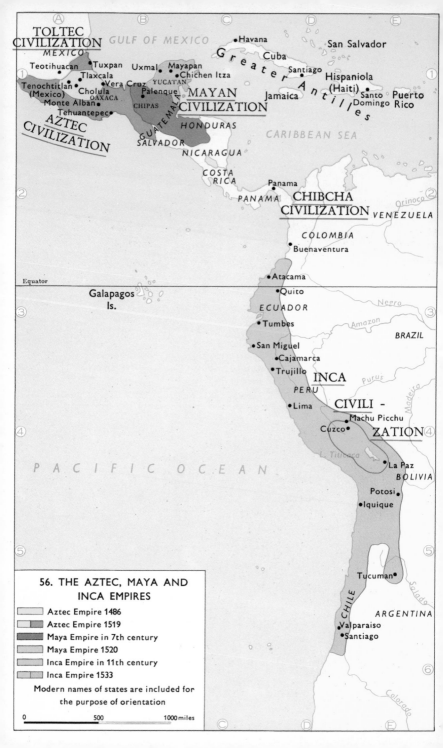

TOLTEC CIVILIZATION
MEXICO
GULF OF MEXICO
• Havana
Cuba
San Salvador
Teotihuacan
• Tuxpan
Uxmal • Mayapan
Cuba
Santiago
Hispaniola (Haiti)
Tlaxcala
• Chichen Itza
Tenochtitlan (Mexico)
Vera Cruz
YUCATAN
Jamaica
Santo Domingo
Puerto Rico
Cholula
• Palenque
MAYAN
OAXACA
CHIPAS
CIVILIZATION
Monte Alban
Tehuantepec
HONDURAS
CARIBBEAN SEA
AZTEC CIVILIZATION
GUATEMALA
SALVADOR
NICARAGUA
COSTA RICA
• Panama
PANAMA
CHIBCHA CIVILIZATION
VENEZUELA
Orinoco
COLOMBIA
• Buenaventura
Equator
• Atacama
• Quito
Galapagos Is.
ECUADOR
Negro
Amazon
BRAZIL
• Tumbes
• San Miguel
• Cajamarca
Purus
• Trujillo
INCA
PERU
CIVILI -
Madeira
• Lima
Machu Picchu
ZATION
Cuzco •
L. Titicaca
• La Paz
BOLIVIA
PACIFIC OCEAN
Potosi •
• Iquique
Tucuman •
Salado
ARGENTINA
CHILE
• Valparaiso
• Santiago
Colorado

56. THE AZTEC, MAYA AND INCA EMPIRES

Aztec Empire 1486
Aztec Empire 1519
Maya Empire in 7th century
Maya Empire 1520
Inca Empire in 11th century
Inca Empire 1533

Modern names of states are included for the purpose of orientation

0   500   1000 miles

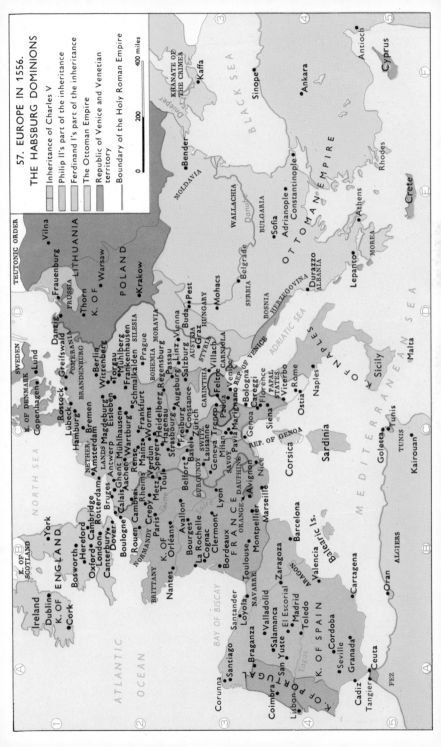

57. EUROPE IN 1556.
THE HABSBURG DOMINIONS

Inheritance of Charles V
Philip II's part of the inheritance
Ferdinand I's part of the inheritance
The Ottoman Empire
Republic of Venice and Venetian territory
Boundary of the Holy Roman Empire

0   200   400 miles

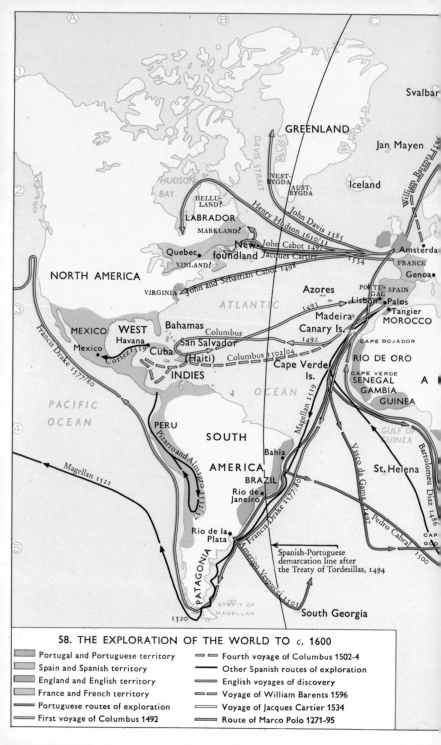

58. THE EXPLORATION OF THE WORLD TO c. 1600

Portugal and Portuguese territory

Spain and Spanish territory

England and English territory

France and French territory

Portuguese routes of exploration

First voyage of Columbus 1492

Fourth voyage of Columbus 1502-4

Other Spanish routes of exploration

English voyages of discovery

Voyage of William Barents 1596

Voyage of Jacques Cartier 1534

Route of Marco Polo 1271-95

Labels on the map:

Svalbar

GREENLAND

Jan Mayen

William Barents 1596

Iceland

HUDSON BAY

NEST-BYGDA
AUST-BYGDA

John Davis 1585

HELLU-LAND?

LABRADOR

MARKLAND?

Henry Hudson 1610/11

New foundland

John Cabot 1497

Amsterdam

Quebec

VINLAND?

Jacques Cartier 1534

FRANCE

Genoa

NORTH AMERICA

John and Sebastian Cabot 1498

VIRGINIA

Azores

PORTU-GAL SPAIN

Lisbon

Palos

ATLANTIC

1493

Madeira

Tangier

MOROCCO

MEXICO

WEST

Bahamas

Columbus

Canary Is.

CAPE BOJADOR

Mexico

Havana

San Salvador

1492

Cortez 1519

Cuba

(Haiti)

Columbus 1502/04

Cape Verde Is.

RIO DE ORO

Francis Drake 1577/80

INDIES

CAPE VERDE

SENEGAL

A

PACIFIC OCEAN

OCEAN

Magellan 1519

GAMBIA

GULF OF GUINEA

GUINEA

PERU

Pizarro and Almagro 1531/3

SOUTH AMERICA

Bahia

Vasco da Gama 1497

St. Helena

Bartolomeu Diaz 1486

Magellan 1521

BRAZIL

Rio de Janeiro

Francis Drake 1577/80

Pedro Cabral 1500

CAP GOO

Rio de la Plata

Spanish-Portuguese demarcation line after the Treaty of Tordesillas, 1494

Americo Vespucci 1501

South Georgia

PATAGONIA

STRAIT OF MAGELLAN

1520

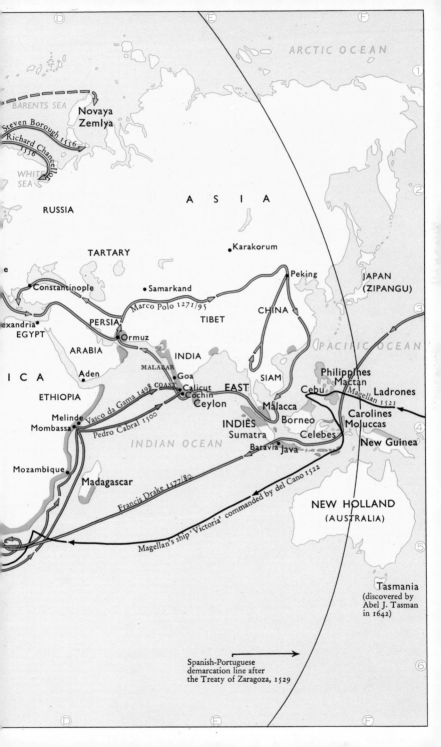

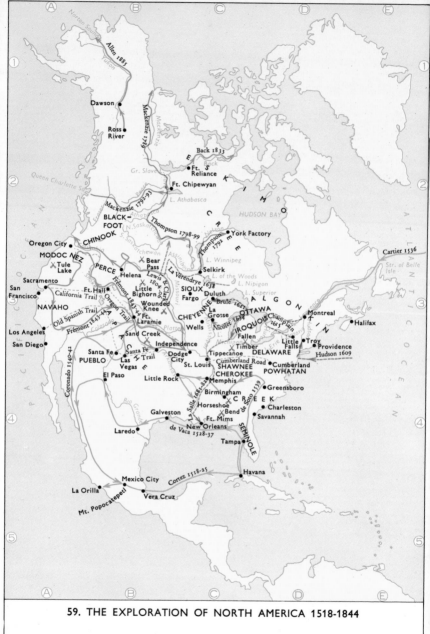

59. THE EXPLORATION OF NORTH AMERICA 1518-1844

APACHE   Indian tribes at time of
            white settlement

X   Battlefields of Indian wars

           16th century exploration

17th century exploration

18th century exploration

19th century exploration

0   200   400   600   800 1000 miles

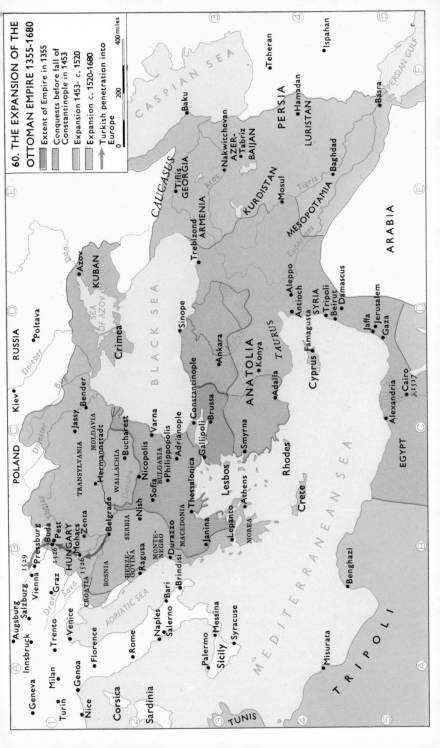

60. THE EXPANSION OF THE OTTOMAN EMPIRE 1355-1680

- Extent of Empire in 1355
- Conquests before fall of Constantinople in 1453
- Expansion 1453- c. 1520
- Expansion c. 1520-1680
- Turkish penetration into Europe

0   200   400 miles

61. THE NETHERLANDS WAR OF INDEPENDENCE

Boundary of the northern provinces which, after the Union of Utrecht in 1579, formed the republic of the United Provinces

<u>Ghent</u> Names underlined indicate towns in the Spanish Netherlands which belonged temporarily to the Union of Utrecht

Catholic Union of Arras 1579

Spanish Netherlands

Church lands

0   20   40   60 miles

62. FRANCE DURING THE HUGUENOT WARS 1562-92

Provinces loyal to the king

Huguenot areas

Provinces supporting the Guises

Spanish territory

0   100   200   300 miles

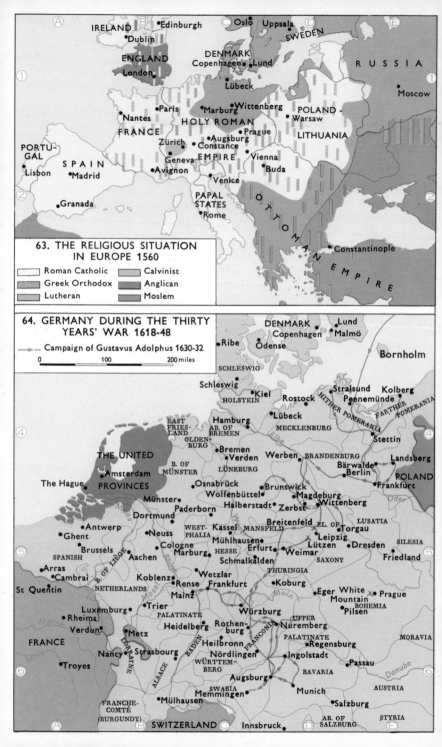

63. THE RELIGIOUS SITUATION IN EUROPE 1560

- Roman Catholic
- Greek Orthodox
- Lutheran
- Calvinist
- Anglican
- Moslem

64. GERMANY DURING THE THIRTY YEARS' WAR 1618-48

→ Campaign of Gustavus Adolphus 1630-32

0   100   200 miles

Map 63 labels

IRELAND
Edinburgh
Dublin
Oslo
Uppsala
SWEDEN
ENGLAND
DENMARK
London
Copenhagen
Lund
Lübeck
RUSSIA
Moscow
Paris
Marburg
Wittenberg
POLAND-
Nantes
HOLY ROMAN
Warsaw
FRANCE
Zürich
Prague
LITHUANIA
PORTU-
GAL
Augsburg
Constance
EMPIRE
Vienna
SPAIN
Geneva
Buda
Lisbon
Madrid
Avignon
Venice
Granada
PAPAL
STATES
Rome
OTTOMAN
EMPIRE
Constantinople

Map 64 labels

DENMARK
Lund
Copenhagen
Malmö
Ribe
Odense
Bornholm
SCHLESWIG
Schleswig
Kiel
Rostock
Stralsund
Kolberg
HOLSTEIN
Peenemünde
HITHER POMERANIA
FARTHER POMERANIA
EAST
FRIES-
LAND
Hamburg
AB. OF
BREMEN
Lübeck
MECKLENBURG
Stettin
OLDEN-
BURG
Bremen
Verden
Werben
BRANDENBURG
THE UNITED
B. OF
MÜNSTER
LÜNEBURG
Bärwalde
Landsberg
Amsterdam
Berlin
POLAND
The Hague
PROVINCES
Osnabrück
Brunswick
Frankfurt
Münster
Wolfenbüttel
Magdeburg
Paderborn
Halberstadt
Zerbst
Wittenberg
Antwerp
Neuss
WEST-
PHALIA
Kassel
MANSFELD
Breitenfeld
EL. OF
LUSATIA
Ghent
Torgau
Dortmund
Mühlhausen
Leipzig
Lützen
Dresden
SILESIA
Brussels
Cologne
Erfurt
Weimar
Aachen
Marburg
HESSE
Schmalkalden
SAXONY
Friedland
Arras
THURINGIA
Cambrai
Koblenz
Wetzlar
Koburg
SPANISH
Rense
Frankfurt
Eger
White
Prague
St Quentin
Mainz
Mountain
NETHERLANDS
BOHEMIA
Luxemburg
Trier
Pilsen
Rheims
PALATINATE
Würzburg
Verdun
Heidelberg
UPPER
FRANCE
Metz
Rothen-
burg
Nuremberg
MORAVIA
Nancy
Strasbourg
BADEN
Heilbronn
PALATINATE
Regensburg
Troyes
Nördlingen
Ingolstadt
Passau
ALSACE
WÜRTTEM-
BERG
FRANCONIA
BAVARIA
FRANCHE-
COMTÉ
(BURGUNDY)
Mülhausen
SWABIA
Augsburg
Memmingen
Munich
Salzburg
AUSTRIA
SWITZERLAND
Innsbruck
AB. OF
SALZBURG
STYRIA
Danube

65. ENGLAND, SCOTLAND AND IRELAND IN THE MID-17TH CENTURY

Areas controlled by Charles I in 1642

Charles I's conquests 1643

Area controlled by Parliament in 1642

Conquests by Parliament in 1643

Area controlled by Parliament in 1645

Areas of Ireland where English and Scottish Protestants were settled during the time of Cromwell

Irish areas given to English settlers c. 1650

0   50   100 miles

THE EDINBURGH AREA

MURRAY
Dundee
FIRTH OF TAY
Kinross • St Andrews
LINDSAY
Loch Leven
Edinburgh • Leith
Craigmillar • Holyrood
Bothwell • Carberry Hill

Orkneys

Hebrides

Dunrobin

MORAY FIRTH

Inverness
MORAY Aberdeen
Balmoral
×Dalnaspidal
Glencoe ×Killiecrankie
ANGUS
SCOTLAND
Perth • Dundee
Stirling
Dunbar
Glasgow Edinburgh
Ayr • Douglas
Turnberry
Dumfries
SOLWAY FIRTH
Carlisle

NORTH SEA

ATLANTIC OCEAN

Londonderry
TYRONE
ULSTER
Belfast

Man

IRISH SEA

CONNAUGHT

Drogheda
Boyne
IRELAND • Dublin
LEINSTER
Limerick
Kilkenny
MUNSTER Wexford
Cork

NORTH-UMBERLAND
Newcastle
Durham
WEST-MORLAND

YORKSHIRE
Lancaster • York
Preston × Leeds Hull
LANCA- Bradford
Manchester
SHIRE ×Gainsborough
Conway Sheffield Lincoln
CHESHIRE NOTTINGHAM
Derby Nottingham
Shrewsbury LEICESTER Norwich
Leicester NORFOLK
ENGLAND
Naseby× Ely
Stratford Cambridge
Worcester Bedford SUFFOLK
Cardigan Edgehill× Harwich
Gloucester Buckingham ESSEX
Pembroke Berkeley Oxford Hatfield
Castle Bristol Reading London
Bath Newbury Greenwich
Sedgemoor SURREY Canterbury
Bridgwater Salisbury KENT Dover
Taunton SOMERSET
DEVON DORSET Southampton SUSSEX BEACHY HEAD
Isle of Wight

Plymouth
CORNWALL
Tor Bay

ENGLISH CHANNEL

66 LONDON c. 1600

0   ½   1   1½ miles

MIDDLESEX
Bethnal Green
Gray's Inn Mile End Bromley
Lincoln's Inn WHITE CHAPEL Stepney
HYDE PARK MAYFAIR St Paul's
LONDON CITY Poplar
Bridge Tower
Kensington Buckingham WEST- Whitehall Globe Theatre
Palace (built 1698) MINSTER Westminster SOUTHWARK
Brompton Abbey Parliament Lambeth
Chelsea Newington
Vauxhall Walworth DEPTFORD GREEN-WICH
Nine Elms SURREY
Thames

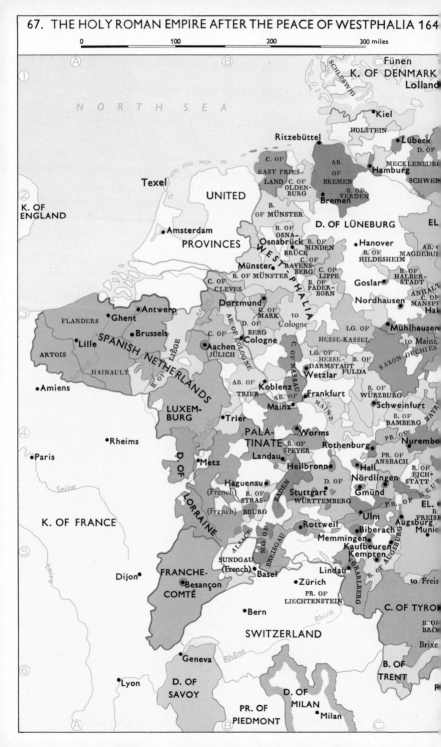

67. THE HOLY ROMAN EMPIRE AFTER THE PEACE OF WESTPHALIA 164[8]

0   100   200   300 miles

NORTH SEA

SCHLESWIG

Fünen

K. OF DENMARK

Lolland

Kiel

HOLSTEIN

Lübeck

D. OF

Ritzebüttel

MECKLENBURG

C. OF
EAST FRIES-
LAND

C. OF
OLDEN-
BURG

AB.
OF
BREMEN

Hamburg

SCHWER[IN]

B. OF
VERDEN

Texel

Bremen

UNITED

D. OF LÜNEBURG

EL[BE]

**K. OF
ENGLAND**

B.
OF MÜNSTER

Amsterdam

PROVINCES

B. OF
OSNA-
BRÜCK

Hanover

AB. OF
MAGDEBU[RG]

Osnabrück

B. OF
MINDEN

B. OF
HILDESHEIM

WESTPHALIA

C. OF
RAVENS-
BERG

B. OF
HALBER-
STADT

Münster

B. OF MÜNSTER

C. OF
LIPPE

Goslar

ANHAL[T]

B. OF
PADER-
BORN

C. OF
MANSFE[LD]

Nordhausen

Hal[LE]

C. OF
CLEVES

Dortmund

Mühlhausen

C. OF
MARK

D. OF
BERG

to
Cologne

LG. OF

FLANDERS

Ghent

Antwerp

AB. OF
COLOGNE

HESSE-KASSEL

to Mainz

Brussels

SPANISH NETHERLANDS

Cologne

Aachen
JÜLICH

C. OF
NASSAU

LG. OF
HESSE-
DARMSTADT

B. OF

SAXON DUCHIES

Lille

B. OF LIÈGE

FULDA

ARTOIS

HAINAULT

AB. OF
TRIER

Koblenz

Frankfurt

B. OF
WÜRZBURG

Amiens

LUXEM-
BURG

AB. OF
MAINZ

Schweinfurt

Trier

Wetzlar

B. OF
BAMBERG

PR. OF
NUREMBE[RG]

Rheims

D. OF

Mainz

MAINZ

PALA-
TINATE

Worms

BAYR[EUTH]

Paris

LORRAINE

Metz

B. OF
SPEYER

Rothenburg

PR. OF
ANSBACH

B. OF
EICH-
STÄTT

Landau

Heilbronn

Hall

NEUB[URG]

K. OF FRANCE

Haguenau
(French)

R. OF
STRAS-
BOURG
(French)

BADEN

D. OF

Stuttgart
WÜRTTEMBERG

Nördlingen

Gmünd

EL[ECTORATE]

B.
FREISI[NG]

Ulm

Augsburg

Munic[H]

Rottweil

Biberach

C. OF
AUGSBURG

ALSACE

MG. OF
BREISGAU

Memmingen

Kaufbeuren

Dijon

SUNDGAU
(French)

Basel

Lindau

Kempten

VORARLBERG

to Freis[ING]

FRANCHE-
COMTÉ

Besançon

Zürich

PR. OF
LIECHTENSTEIN

C. OF TYRO[L]

Bern

SWITZERLAND

Rhine

B. OF
BRIX[EN]

Brixe[N]

Geneva

Rhône

B. OF
TRENT

Lyon

D. OF
SAVOY

D. OF
MILAN

R[...]

PR. OF
PIEDMONT

Milan

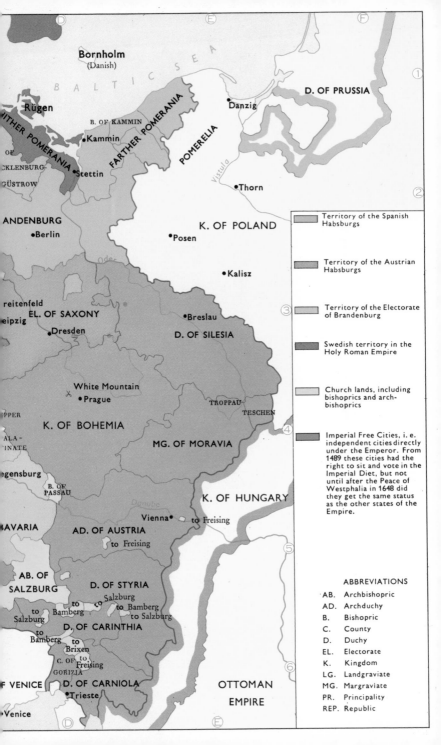

Bornholm
(Danish)

BALTIC SEA

Rügen

HITHER POMERANIA

OF
CKLENBURG-
GÜSTROW

●Stettin

●Kammin

B. OF KAMMIN

FARTHER POMERANIA

POMERELIA

Danzig●

D. OF PRUSSIA

Vistula

●Thorn

ANDENBURG

●Berlin

K. OF POLAND

●Posen

Oder

●Kalisz

reitenfeld
eipzig

EL. OF SAXONY

●Dresden

●Breslau

D. OF SILESIA

TROPPAU

TESCHEN

PPER

ALA-
INATE

White Mountain
✕ ●Prague

K. OF BOHEMIA

MG. OF MORAVIA

egensburg

B. OF
PASSAU

Danube

K. OF HUNGARY

AVARIA

Vienna● to Freising

AD. OF AUSTRIA
to Freising

AB. OF
SALZBURG

to Salzburg
to Bamberg

D. OF STYRIA

to Salzburg
to Salzburg

Salzburg
Bamberg

to
Bamberg

D. OF CARINTHIA
to
Brixen

C. OF to Freising
GORIZIA

F VENICE

D. OF CARNIOLA
●Trieste

OTTOMAN

EMPIRE

●Venice

	Territory of the Spanish Habsburgs
	Territory of the Austrian Habsburgs
	Territory of the Electorate of Brandenburg
	Swedish territory in the Holy Roman Empire
	Church lands, including bishoprics and arch-bishoprics
	Imperial Free Cities, i. e. independent cities directly under the Emperor. From 1489 these cities had the right to sit and vote in the Imperial Diet, but not until after the Peace of Westphalia in 1648 did they get the same status as the other states of the Empire.

ABBREVIATIONS

AB.   Archbishopric
AD.   Archduchy
B.   Bishopric
C.   County
D.   Duchy
EL.   Electorate
K.   Kingdom
LG.   Landgraviate
MG.   Margraviate
PR.   Principality
REP. Republic

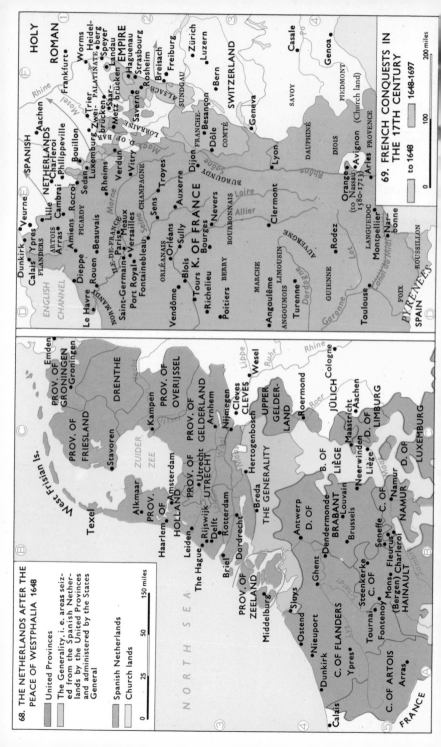

70. NORTHEASTERN EUROPE IN 1660: EXPANSION OF SWEDEN IN 17TH CENT.

Sweden at the death of Gustavus Vasa, 1560
Conquests 1561-1660
Conquered from Denmark-Norway 1645-60
Duchy of Holstein-Gottorp
Dates show the year of conquest
● Fortresses   Sw. Swedish

0   100   200   300 miles

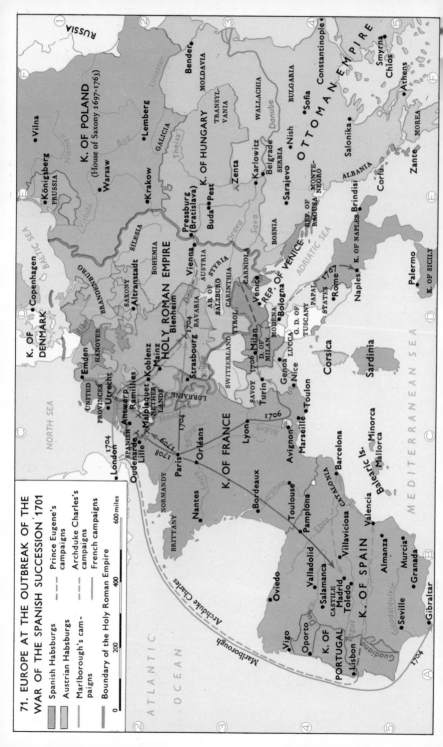

71. EUROPE AT THE OUTBREAK OF THE WAR OF THE SPANISH SUCCESSION, 1701

Spanish Habsburgs
Austrian Habsburgs
Marlborough's campaigns
Prince Eugene's campaigns
Archduke Charles's campaigns
French campaigns
Boundary of the Holy Roman Empire

0 200 400 600 miles

ATLANTIC OCEAN

RUSSIA

K. OF POLAND
(House of Saxony 1697-1763)

•Vilna
•Königsberg PRUSSIA
•Warsaw
•Krakow
•Lemberg
•Bender

MOLDAVIA
GALICIA
TRANSYLVANIA
WALLACHIA

K. OF HUNGARY
Pressburg (Bratislava)
Buda •Pest
xZenta
xKarlowitz
Belgrade SERBIA
•Sarajevo
BOSNIA
REP. OF RAGUSA

OTTOMAN EMPIRE
•Nish
•Sofia
BULGARIA
•Constantinople
•Smyrna
Chios•
•Athens
MOREA
Zante•
SALONIKA
ALBANIA
Corfu•

HOLY ROMAN EMPIRE
BOHEMIA
Altranstadt•
SAXONY
SILESIA
BRANDENBURG
HANOVER
•Emden
Mainz•
Koblenz•
Blenheim 1704
BAVARIA
Vienna• AUSTRIA
STYRIA
AB. OF SALZBURG
CARINTHIA
CARNIOLA
TYROL

K. OF DENMARK
•Copenhagen
BALTIC SEA
NORTH SEA

UNITED PROVINCES
Antwerp•
Utrecht•
SPANISH NETHER-LANDS
Ramillies x
Oudenarde x 1708
Malplaquet x 1709
Lille• 1708
•London 1704

Strasbourg•
LORRAINE
SWITZERLAND

K. OF FRANCE
Paris•
Orléans•
Nantes•
BRITTANY
NORMANDY
Bordeaux•
Toulouse•
Lyon• 1706
Avignon•
Marseille•
Toulon•
Nice•
SAVOY
Turin•
D. OF MILAN
Milan•
Genoa•
G. D. OF TUSCANY
LUCCA
MODENA
REP. OF VENICE
Venice•
Bologna•
PAPAL STATES
Rome• 1707
K. OF NAPLES
Naples•
Brindisi•
ADRIATIC SEA
Palermo•
K. OF SICILY

Corsica
Sardinia

K. OF SPAIN
CASTILE
Madrid•
Toledo•
Salamanca•
Valladolid•
Oviedo•
Vigo•
Oporto•
K. OF PORTUGAL
Lisbon•
Seville•
Granada•
Murcia•
Almanza•
Villaviciosa•
Valencia•
Barcelona•
CATALONIA
Pamplona•
Gibraltar• 1704

Balearic Is.
Minorca•
Mallorca•

MEDITERRANEAN SEA

Marlborough 1704
Archduke Charles 1704

72. THE EXPANSION OF RUSSIA FROM 1300 TO 1825

Principality of Moscow c. 1300
Grand Duchy of Moscow 1462
Conquests of the Rurik dynasty 1462-1605. Areas subsequently lost are outlined

Expansion between 1643 and 1676
Expansion under Peter the Great 1682-1725
Expansion under Empress Anna 1730-40. Areas subsequently lost are outlined

Expansion under Empress Elizabeth 1741-62
Expansion under Catherine the Great 1762-96
Expansion up to death of Alexander I 1825

0   200   400 miles

ARCTIC OCEAN
NORTH CAPE
LAPLAND
NORWAY
SWEDEN
WHITE SEA
FINLAND
Archangel
Onega
GULF OF BOTHNIA
Nystad
Åbo
Viborg
KARELIA
Ladoga
Onega
Kronstadt
Schlüsselburg(Nöteborg)
Åland Is.
Narva
St Petersburg
Visby
Dagö
ESTONIA
INGRIA
Novgorod
Ösel
L. Peipus
BALTIC SEA
LIVONIA
NOVGOROD
Uglitch
KHANATE OF
Riga
Kazan
KOURLAND
Dvina
Viatka
Danzig
Vilna
Moscow
Nizhni-Novgorod
PRUSSIA
Oka
KAZAN
Thorn
LITHUANIA
Holovzin
Smolensk
Kama
Minsk
Andrussov
Tula
Warsaw
Lesna
Polish
Volga
POLAND
Pripet
1611-67
Ural
Krakow
MARSHES
Kiev
GALICIA
UKRAINE
Kharkov
Don
(LITTLE RUSSIA)
Poltava
HUNGARY
Prut
Perevolotchna
Jassy
MOLDAVIA
Bender
Dniester
Bug
Dnieper
Azov
KHANATE OF
Astrakhan
TRANSYLVANIA
KHANATE OF THE CRIMEA
ASTRAKHAN
WALLACHIA
Danube
CRIMEA
SEA OF AZOV
Kuban
CASPIAN SEA
Sofia
Sevastopol
Kaffa (Feodosiya)
Varna
BLACK SEA
CAUCASUS
Terek
Adrianople
Tiflis
Kura
Constantinople
Batum
Ardakhan
Baku
OTTOMAN EMPIRE
Kars
Aras
Euphrates
Tigris
PERSIA

73. CAMPAIGN OF CHARLES XII 1700-09

Swedish territory at outbreak of Northern War 1700

Charles's campaign. The vertical strokes indicate the beginning of a year

Charles's journey to Stralsund

0   200   400 miles

74. LITHUANIA AND POLAND 13TH-14TH CENTURIES

Lithuania 1263

Expansion 1316-41

Lithuania at the time of union with Poland 1386

Expansion of Lithuania 1392-1430

Poland 1340

Poland at the time of union with Lithuania 1386

0   200   400 miles

Map 73 labels

Stavanger
Christiania
Uppsala
Åland
Reval
Narva
Novgorod
K. OF SWEDEN
Stockholm
ESTONIA
Dorpat
Göteborg
Gotland
LIVONIA
Moscow
Aarhus
Karlshamn
Libau
Riga
Copenhagen
BALTIC SEA
Smolensk
Kovno
Vilna
Smorgon
Holovzin
Tønning
Bornholm
Königsberg
PRUSSIA
Mogilev
Hamburg
Stralsund
arrived 10-11 Nov. 1714
Danzig
Elbing
Grodno
Minsk
Lesna
RUSSIA
Bremen
HAN-OVER
BRANDENBURG
Berlin
Fraustadt
Warsaw
K. OF POLAND
Kharkov
Cologne
Kassel
SAXONY 1707
Altranstadt
SILESIA
Kiev
Poltava
1709
Perevolotchna
Chigirin
Charles's flight
HOLY ROMAN EMPIRE
Krakow
Lemberg
BAVARIA
Vienna
AUSTRIA
K. OF HUNGARY
Bender 1709/13
Otchakov
SWITZERLAND
CRIMEA
Pitesti departed 27 Oct. 1712
BLACK SEA
OTTOMAN EMPIRE
Demotika 1713/14
Danube
Rhine
Dniester
Dnieper
Oka
Volga
Dvina
Niemen

Map 74 labels

BALTIC SEA
Libau
TEUTONIC ORDER
Memel
Moscow
Bornholm
Teutonic order 1398-1411
EAST PRUSSIA
Königsberg
Vilna
Smolensk
RUSSIA
WEST PRUSSIA
Danzig
Polish 1466
Marienburg
Polish feudal dependent 1466
LITHUANIA
Andrussov
Tannenberg
Minsk
Thorn
MASOVIA
Posen
POLAND
Warsaw
Brest
Pinsk
Liegnitz
Rava
Breslau
SILESIA
Lublin
Pripet
Czestochowa
Kiev
MORAVIA
Krakow
Wieliczka
UKRAINE
GALICIA
Lemberg
Warta
Niemen
Bug
Dniester
Dnieper
SEA OF AZOV
1386

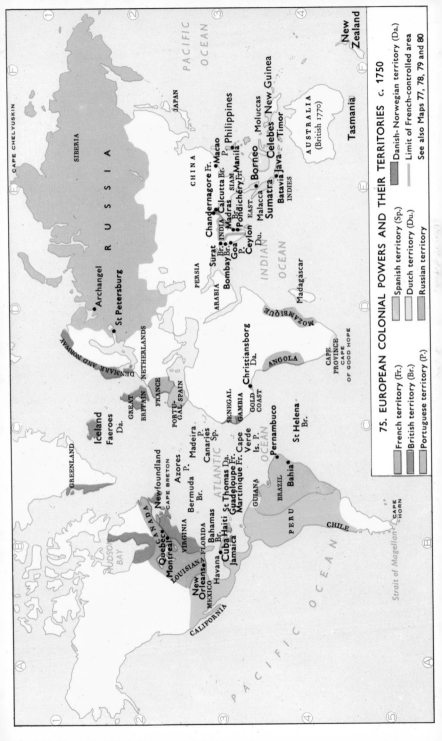

75. EUROPEAN COLONIAL POWERS AND THEIR TERRITORIES c. 1750

French territory (Fr.)

British territory (Br.)

Portuguese territory (P.)

Spanish territory (Sp.)

Dutch territory (Du.)

Russian territory

Danish-Norwegian territory (Da.)

Limit of French-controlled area

See also Maps 77, 78, 79 and 80

CAPE CHELYUSKIN

PACIFIC OCEAN

New Zealand

Tasmania

SIBERIA

RUSSIA

JAPAN

CHINA

Macao Fr.

Chandernagore Fr.

Calcutta Br.

INDIA

Madras Br.

Pondicherry Fr.

SIAM

Philippines

Manila P.

Moluccas

New Guinea

Celebes

Borneo

EAST INDIES

Malacca

Batavia Du.

Java

Timor

Sumatra

Ceylon Du.

Goa P.

Bombay Br.

Surat

ARABIA

PERSIA

INDIAN OCEAN

Madagascar

MOZAMBIQUE

AUSTRALIA (British 1770)

Archangel

St Petersburg

DENMARK AND NORWAY

NETHERLANDS

GREAT BRITAIN

FRANCE

PORTU-GAL SPAIN

Iceland Da.

Faeroes Da.

GREENLAND

ANGOLA

Christiansborg Da.

CAPE PROVINCE

CAPE OF GOOD HOPE

SENEGAL

GAMBIA

GOLD COAST

St Helena Br.

PACIFIC OCEAN

ATLANTIC OCEAN

Madeira P.

Azores P.

Canaries Sp.

Cape Verde Is. P.

Bermuda Br.

St Thomas Da.

Guadeloupe Fr.

Martinique Fr.

Bahamas Br.

Cuba Haiti

Jamaica Br.

Havana

MEXICO

CALIFORNIA

Mexico

New Orleans

LOUISIANA

VIRGINIA

FLORIDA

Quebec

Montreal

CANADA

CAPE BRETON

Newfoundland

HUDSON BAY

GUIANA

Pernambuco

BRAZIL P.

Bahia

PERU

CHILE

Strait of Magellan

CAPE HORN

76. EUROPE IN 1721

Austrian territory

British territory including Hanover, united under the same king 1714-1837

Brandenburg territory

Swedish territory

Boundary of Holy Roman Empire

0   200   400 miles

Shetland Is.

Orkney Is.

Hebrides

Bergen

Stavanger

NORTH SEA

OF DENMARK AND NORWAY

Culloden
Aberdeen
SCOTLAND
Scone
Falkirk
Glasgow   Edinburgh
Berwick
Belfast
Newcastle
K. OF GREAT BRITAIN
IRELAND   Dublin
Ripon
York
Limerick
Newark
Cork   Wexford   Derby
Newmark
ENGLAND   Southwold
Worcester   Cambridge
Oxford
Exeter   London
Chatham
Plymouth   Portland   Dover
Dunkirk

UNITED
Amsterdam
The Hague   Utrecht
PROVINCES   Münste
Ostend   Cologne
AUSTRIAN   Aachen
Fontenoy
NETHER-
CAP DE LA   Cambrai   LANDS
HOGUE   Rouen
Rhine
Brest   Rheims
LOR-   Rastatt
Versailles   Paris   Nancy   Cirey   Stra
Fontainebleau   RAINE
Nantes   Orléans   Seine   Basel
Tours
K. OF FRANCE   Ferney   SWITZER
Rochefort   Geneva
Limoges   Lyon   SAVOY
Bordeaux   Turin
Garonne   REP
Oviedo   Bayonne   Toulouse   Avignon
Pamplona   Montpellier   Marseille
Burgos   Toulon
Oporto   Valladolid
Ebro   Zaragoza
K. OF SPAIN   Barcelona
Madrid
Duero   Toledo
Lisbon   Tagus   Valencia   Minorca
K. OF PORTUGAL   (British 1703-83)
Almanza   Mallorca
Guadiana   Balearic Is.
Guadalquivir
Seville
Cadiz   Granada   Cartagena
Gibraltar   MEDITERRANEA
(British 1713)

BARBARY STATES

ATLANTIC OCEAN

Tor Bay

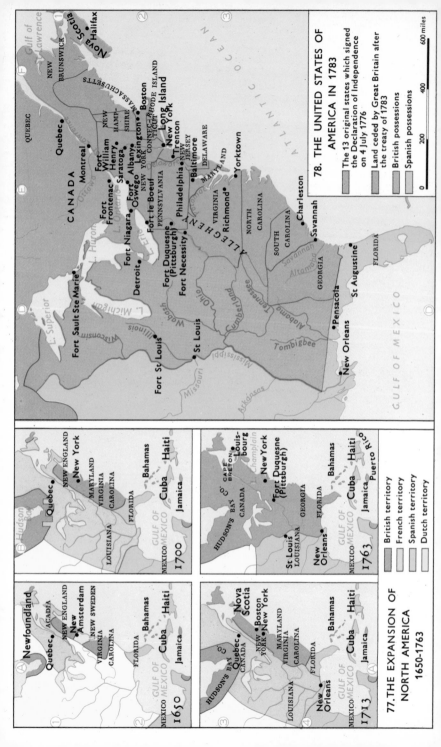

78. THE UNITED STATES OF AMERICA IN 1783

The 13 original states which signed the Declaration of Independence on 4 July 1776

Land ceded by Great Britain after the treaty of 1783

British possessions

Spanish possessions

0   200   400   600 miles

Map 78 labels:

Gulf of St. Lawrence
NOVA SCOTIA
Halifax
NEW BRUNSWICK
QUEBEC
CANADA
Quebec
Montreal
Fort William Henry
Saratoga
Fort Frontenac
Albany
Fort Niagara
Oswego
Fort-le Boeuf
Detroit
Fort Duquesne (Pittsburgh)
Fort Necessity
L. Superior
Fort Sault Ste Marie
L. Huron
L. Michigan
L. Ontario
L. Erie
Fort St Louis
St Louis
NEW HAMPSHIRE
MASSACHUSETTS
Boston
Lexington
RHODE ISLAND
CONNECTICUT
Long Island
New York
NEW YORK
Trenton
NEW JERSEY
PENNSYLVANIA
Philadelphia
Baltimore
DELAWARE
MARYLAND
VIRGINIA
Richmond
Yorktown
ALLEGHENY
NORTH CAROLINA
SOUTH CAROLINA
Charleston
GEORGIA
Savannah
FLORIDA
St Augustine
Pensacola
New Orleans
ATLANTIC OCEAN
GULF OF MEXICO
Missouri
Mississippi
Arkansas
Ohio
Wabash
Illinois
Wisconsin
Tennessee
Cumberland
Tombigbee
Alabama
Altamaha
Savannah

77. THE EXPANSION OF NORTH AMERICA 1650-1763

British territory
French territory
Spanish territory
Dutch territory

1650
Newfoundland
ACADIA
Quebec
NEW ENGLAND
New Amsterdam
NEW SWEDEN
NEW YORK
MARYLAND
VIRGINIA
CAROLINA
FLORIDA
Bahamas
Cuba
Haiti
Jamaica
GULF OF MEXICO
MEXICO
LOUISIANA

1700
Hudson Bay
Quebec
NEW ENGLAND
New York
MARYLAND
VIRGINIA
CAROLINA
FLORIDA
Bahamas
Cuba
Haiti
Jamaica
GULF OF MEXICO
MEXICO
LOUISIANA

1713
HUDSON'S BAY CO.
CANADA
Quebec
Nova Scotia
Boston
New York
NEW ENGLAND
MARYLAND
VIRGINIA
CAROLINA
FLORIDA
New Orleans
LOUISIANA
Bahamas
Cuba
Haiti
Jamaica
GULF OF MEXICO
MEXICO

1763
HUDSON'S BAY CO.
CANADA
CAPE BRETON CO.
Louisbourg
Lake Champlain
Fort Duquesne (Pittsburgh)
New York
GEORGIA
FLORIDA
St Louis
LOUISIANA
New Orleans
Bahamas
Cuba
Haiti
Jamaica
Puerto Rico
GULF OF MEXICO
MEXICO

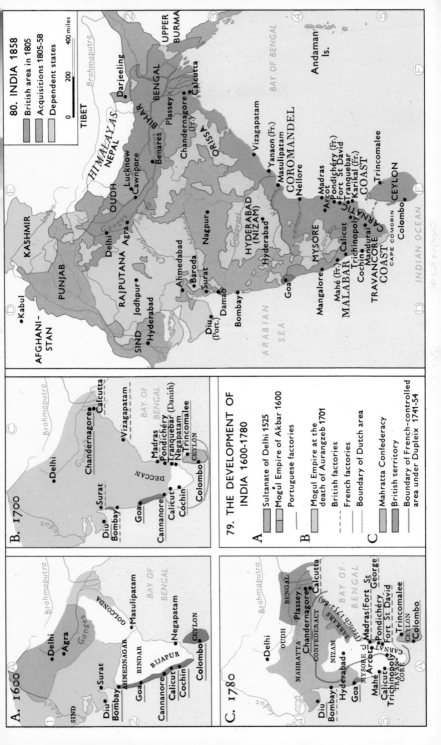

80. INDIA 1858

- British area in 1805
- Acquisitions 1805-58
- Dependent states

0   200   400 miles

D. 1858

AFGHANISTAN
Kabul
KASHMIR
PUNJAB
SIND
Hyderabad
RAJPUTANA
Jodhpur
Delhi
Agra
HIMALAYAS
NEPAL
TIBET
Brahmaputra
Darjeeling
OUDH
Lucknow
Cawnpore
BENGAL
BIHAR
Benares
Calcutta
Plassey
Chandernagore (Fr.)
ORISSA
Ahmedabad
Baroda
Surat
Bombay
Damao
Diu (Port.)
Nagpur
Narbada
Godavari
HYDERABAD (NIZAM)
Hyderabad
Goa
ARABIAN SEA
Vizagapatam
Yanaon (Fr.)
Masulipatam
COROMANDEL COAST
Nellore
MYSORE
Mangalore
Cauvery
Calicut
MALABAR COAST
Mahé (Fr.)
Cochin
TRAVANCORE COAST
Trichinopoly
Madurai
CARNATIC
Madras
Arcot
Pondichéry (Fr.)
Fort St David
Karikal (Fr.)
Tranquebar
CAPE COMORIN
CEYLON
Colombo
Trincomalee
INDIAN OCEAN
BAY OF BENGAL
Andaman Is.
UPPER BURMA

B. 1700

Brahmaputra
Indus
Ganges
Delhi
Surat
Diu
Bombay
Goa
Cannanore
Calicut
Cochin
CEYLON
Colombo
DECCAN
Chandernagore
Calcutta
Vizagapatam
BAY OF BENGAL
Madras
Pondichéry
Tranquebar (Danish)
Negapatam
Trincomalee

79. THE DEVELOPMENT OF INDIA 1600-1780

A
- Sultanate of Delhi 1525
- Mogul Empire of Akbar 1600
- Portuguese factories

B
- Mogul Empire at the death of Aurangzeb 1701
- British factories
- French factories
- Boundary of Dutch area

C
- Mahratta Confederacy
- British territory
- Boundary of French-controlled area under Dupleix 1741-54

A. 1600

Indus
Ganges
Brahmaputra
SIND
Delhi
Agra
Surat
Diu
Bombay
AHMEDNAGAR
BIJAPUR
BIDAR
GOLCONDA
Masulipatam
Goa
Cannanore
Calicut
Cochin
Negapatam
CEYLON
Colombo
BAY OF BENGAL

C. 1780

Brahmaputra
Indus
Delhi
OUDH
BENGAL
Chandernagore
Calcutta
Plassey
MAHRATTA CONFEDERACY
NIZAM
Hyderabad
Bombay
Diu
Goa
Mahé
Calicut
MYSORE
TRAVANCORE
Trichinopoly
CARNATIC
Arcot
Madras (Fort St George)
Pondichéry
Fort St David
NORTHERN CIRCARS (French 1753-66)
BAY OF BENGAL
Trincomalee
CEYLON
Colombo

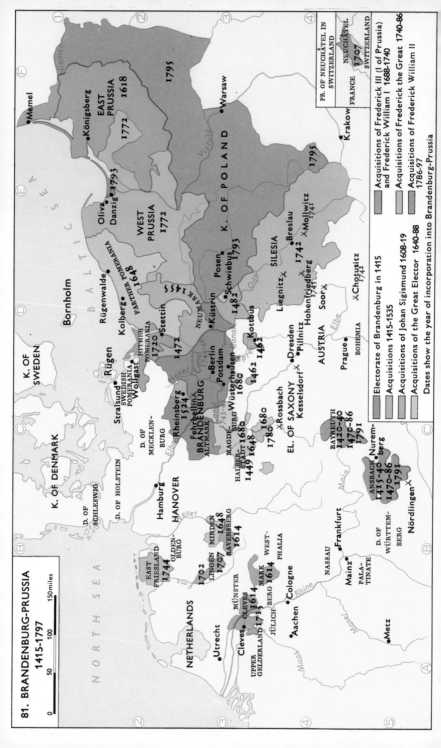

81. BRANDENBURG-PRUSSIA
1415-1797

0   50   100   150 miles

Legend:

Electorate of Brandenburg in 1415
Acquisitions 1415-1535
Acquisitions of Johan Sigismund 1608-19
Acquisitions of the Great Elector 1640-88

Acquisitions of Frederick III (I of Prussia) and Frederick William I 1688-1740
Acquisitions of Frederick the Great 1740-86
Acquisitions of Frederick William II 1786-97

Dates show the year of incorporation into Brandenburg-Prussia

PR. OF NEUCHÂTEL IN SWITZERLAND

NEUCHÂTEL 1707

SWITZERLAND

FRANCE

K. OF SWEDEN

NORTH SEA

BALTIC SEA

Bornholm

K. OF DENMARK

D. OF SCHLESWIG

D. OF HOLSTEIN

Memel

East Prussia 1618

Königsberg

1772

Oliva 1793

Danzig

West Prussia 1772

Warsaw

K. OF POLAND

Posen 1793

Krakow

Silesia

Breslau

Mollwitz 1741

1742

Liegnitz

Soor

Hohenfriedberg 1745

Chotusitz 1742

Schwiebus 1482

Küstrin

Kottbus 1462

Stettin

Farther Pomerania 1648

Rügenwalde

Kolberg

Rügen

Stralsund

Swedish Pomerania

Wolgast

Hither Pomerania 1720

Neumark 1455

Berlin

Potsdam

Wüstenhausen 1680

Brandenburg

Altmark

Fehrbellin

Rheinsberg 1524

Magdeburg 1680

Halberstadt 1648

1449

1462   1462

1648

1680

1780

Rossbach

Kesselsdorf

El. OF SAXONY

Dresden

Pillnitz

Prague

BOHEMIA

AUSTRIA

Elbe

D. OF MECKLENBURG

Hamburg

HANOVER

Weser

Minden 1648

Ravensberg 1614

Oldenburg

Lingen 1702

East Friesland 1744

Münster

Cleves 1614

Upper Gelderland 1713

Jülich   Berg

Mark 1614

WESTPHALIA

Cologne

Aachen

Utrecht

NETHERLANDS

Rhine

Maas

Frankfurt

NASSAU

Mainz

PALATINATE

Metz

Maine

D. OF WÜRTTEMBERG

Nordlingen

Ansbach 1415-40   1470-86   1791

Bayreuth 1420-40   1470-86   1791

Nuremberg

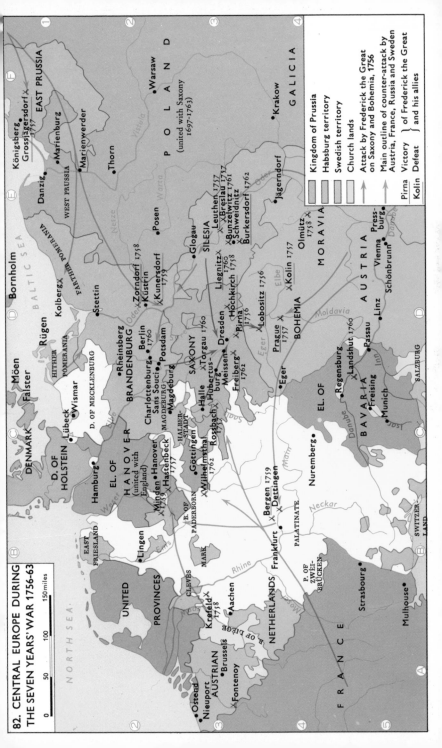

82. CENTRAL EUROPE DURING THE SEVEN YEARS' WAR 1756-63

0   50   100   150 miles

Legend:
- Kingdom of Prussia
- Habsburg territory
- Swedish territory
- Church lands
- Attack by Frederick the Great on Saxony and Bohemia, 1756
- Main outline of counter-attack by Austria, France, Russia and Sweden
- Pirna — Victory } of Frederick the Great
- Kolin — Defeat } and his allies

NORTH SEA

BALTIC SEA

Bornholm

Möen
Falster
Rügen

DENMARK

D. OF HOLSTEIN

Hamburg
Lübeck
Wismar

D. OF MECKLENBURG

HITHER POMERANIA
FARTHER POMERANIA

Kolberg×
Stettin

Königsberg
Grossjägersdorf× 1757
EAST PRUSSIA

Danzig
Marienburg
Marienwerder

WEST PRUSSIA

Warsaw

Thorn

Posen

POLAND
(united with Saxony 1697-1763)

Krakow

GALICIA

UNITED PROVINCES

EAST FRIESLAND

Lingen

EL. OF HANOVER
(united with England)

Hanover
Minden× 1759
Hastenbeck× 1757
Göttingen

B. OF PADERBORN
Wilhelmsthal× 1762

MARK

CLEVES

Krefeld× 1758
Aachen

P. OF LIÈGE

AUSTRIAN NETHERLANDS

Ostend
Nieuport
Brussels
Fontenoy×

Dettingen
Frankfurt
Bergen 1759×

PALATINATE
P. OF ZWEI-BRÜCKEN

Nuremberg

Neckar

Rhine

Maas

Strasbourg

Mulhouse

FRANCE

SWITZERLAND

Rheinsberg
Charlottenburg
Sans Souci
Potsdam
Berlin 1760

BRANDENBURG

Küstrin
Zorndorf 1758×
Kunersdorf× 1759

Glogau

SILESIA

Breslau× 1757
Leuthen× 1757
Liegnitz× 1760
Bunzelwitz 1761
Schweidnitz 1761
Burkersdorf 1762

Jägerndorf

Oder

Warta

Vistula

Netze

HALBERSTADT
Halle
Magdeburg
MAGDEBURG
Rossbach× 1757
Hubertusburg

SAXONY

Dresden
Meissen
Torgau 1760×
Freiberg× 1761
Pirna 1756
Hochkirch× 1758

BOHEMIA

Prague 1757×
Lobositz 1756×
Kolin 1757×
Eger

Elbe
Eger
Moldavia

MORAVIA

Olmütz 1758×

AUSTRIA

Linz
Vienna
Pressburg
Schönbrunn

Danube

EL. OF BAVARIA

Regensburg
Landshut 1760×
Freising×
Munich

Passau
Inn
Isar

SALZBURG

Weser
Ems
Main
Saal

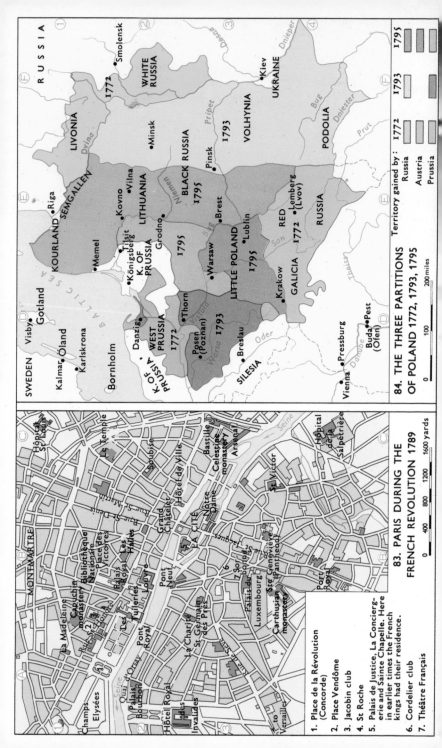

83. PARIS DURING THE FRENCH REVOLUTION 1789

1. Place de la Révolution (Concorde)
2. Place Vendôme
3. Jacobin club
4. St Roche
5. Palais de Justice, La Conciergerie and Sainte Chapelle. Here in earlier times the French kings had their residence.
6. Cordelier club
7. Théâtre Français

0 400 800 1200 1600 yards

84. THE THREE PARTITIONS OF POLAND 1772, 1793, 1795

Territory gained by:
Russia
Austria
Prussia

1772　1793　1795

0　100　200 miles

85. ITALY c. 1800

French territory:
- France 1792
- Piedmont, seized from Sardinia 1798
- Duchy of Parma, seized 1803

States under French control:
- Cisalpine Republic 1797-1802, Italian Republic 1802-05
- Ligurian Republic 1797-1805
- Papal States, Roman Republic 1797-1805
- Republic of Lucca 1799-1805
- K. of Naples (Parthenopean Republic) 1799
- K. of Etruria 1801-08
- Pr. of Piombino 1801
- K. of Italy 1805

- K. of Sardinia before 1798
- Rep. of Venice, Austrian 1797-1805

0   100   200 miles

86. EUROPE IN NAPOLEON'S TIME 1812

Legend:
- French territory
- States ruled by Members of Napoleon's family
- Other French-controlled areas
- Allies of France
- Great Britain and British territory
- Neutral states
- --- Napoleon's Eastern campaign 1798
- —— Wellington's Spanish camp. 1808-9
- —— Napoleon's Russian campaign 1812

0   200   400 miles

ATLANTIC OCEAN

NORTH SEA

ENGLISH CHANNEL

MEDITERRANEAN

Bergen
Tran
Christiania
Toverud
Prestebakk
Christians
Göteborg
Fladst

Hälsingb
Copenhage
Kiel
MECK

SCOTLAND
Glasgow
Edinburgh
Belfast
K. OF GREAT BRITAIN
IRELAND Dublin
Manchester
Liverpool
ENGLAND
Birmingham

HOLLAND
K. OF
WEST-
PHALIA
Amsterdam
CON
L

Old Sarum
Bristol London
Plymouth Dover
Southampton
Boulogne Calais
Ghent
Antwerp
Brussels
Aix-la-
Chapelle
Waterloo
Ligny
Gross-Görsche
Auerstädt
Erfurt
K. OF
SAXONY
Karlsba
FEDERAT
OF TH

Eu
Brest
Rouen
Amiens
Koblenz
Châtillon
Malmaison
Rheims
Paris
Varennes
Hambach
Versailles Saint-Cloud
Verdun
K. OF
WÜRTTEM-
BERG
K. OF
Munic
Fontainebleau
Orléans
Brienne
Lunéville
Chaumont
BADEN
Ettenheim
Hohenlinden
Nantes
VENDÉE
FRENCH
EMPIRE
Basel
HELVETIAN
Zürich
Bern
REPUBLIC
BAVA
RHINE

Cape
Finisterre
✕
(1805)

Bordeaux
Lyon
Geneva
Milan
K. OF
Verona
Venice
Oviedo
Bayonne
Vitoria
Toulouse
Montpellier
Turin
Savona
Parma
Genoa
ITAL
Nice
Cannes
LUCCA
Flor
Oporto (1808)
Marseille
Toulon
K. OF
PORTUGAL
Fuentes de Onoro
ANDORRA
Zaragoza
Barcelona
Elba
PIOMBIN
Cintra
Torres Vedras
Lisbon
Talavera
(1809)
Madrid (1808)
Toledo
Corsica
Ajaccio
Rome
K. OF SPAIN
Valencia
Balearic Is.
Minorca
(Br. 1798-1802)
Mallorca
K. OF
SARDINIA
Cagliari
Bailen
Seville
Cartagena
Cadiz
Gibraltar
✕ Cape
Trafalgar
(1805)
Ceuta
Oran
Algiers
Constantine
Tunis
Pale
MOROCCO
ALGERIA
TUNIS
TRIPO

Duero
Guadalquivir
Garonne
Rhône

K. OF DENMARK AND NORWAY

K. OF

FINLAND •Viborg

•Åbo •Helsingfors •St Petersburg
•Sveaborg
•Åland •Reval •Novgorod
•Stockholm ESTONIA

SWEDEN Gotland LIVONIA
•Riga •Borodino •Moscow
Öland KOURLAND
•Vitebsk
arlskrona •Smolensk
nholm Dvina
•Tilsit R U S S I A N
•Königsberg •Vilna
REP. OF •Friedland
DANZIG •Eylau
Niemen
OF PRUSSIA Bremen

rlin •Posen Vistula •Warsaw
•Trachenberg E M P I R E
Bautzen WARSAW
esden •Münchengrätz •Krakow GALICIA •Kiev
Prague
BOHEMIA •Troppau
Brünn MORAVIA
(Brno)
usterlitz A U S T R I A N Dniester
•Aspern •Wagram
Vienna •Essling BESSARABIA
önbrunn •Pressburg MOLDAVIA •Odessa
•Buda •Pest

E M P I R E TRANSYLVANIA CRIMEA
SLOVENIA
•Agram
Laibach SLAVONIA BANAT WALLACHIA B L A C K   S E A
ILLYRIAN PROVINCES BOSNIA •Belgrade •Bucharest
SERBIA Danube

BULGARIA
K. OF MONTE- •Sofia
NEGRO •Adrianople
NTECORVO O RUMELIA
BENEVENTO •Constantinople
Naples T
•Salerno ALBANIA •Salonika
NAPLES T
Corfu O •Lemnos E M P I R E
(French) M
I o n i a n   I s . A
1797 Fr., 1799 Russ., 1809 Br. N •Chios
K. OF
SICILY MOREA •Athens
•Navarino •Rhodes Cyprus

Malta Crete
SYRIA
N •Acre

S E A •Jaffa

•Aboukir
•Alexandria
•Cairo
EGYPT

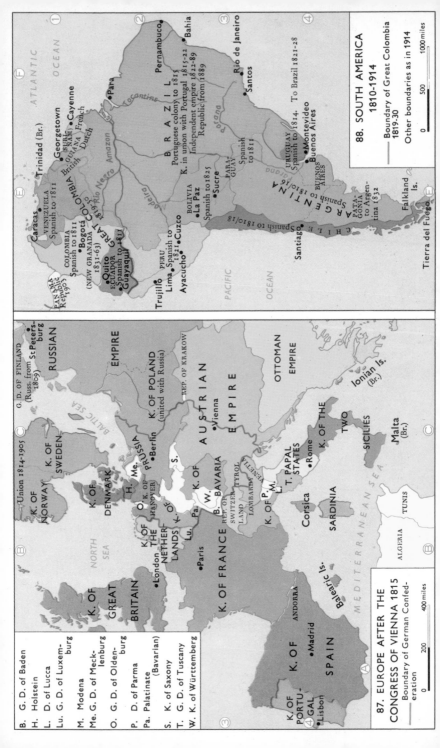

87. EUROPE AFTER THE CONGRESS OF VIENNA 1815

Boundary of German Confederation

0   200   400 miles

B. G. D. of Baden
H. Holstein
L. D. of Lucca
Lu. G. D. of Luxemburg
M. Modena
Me. G. D. of Mecklenburg
O. G. D. of Oldenburg
P. D. of Parma
Pa. Palatinate (Bavarian)
S. K. of Saxony
T. G. D. of Tuscany
W. K. of Württemberg

G. D. OF FINLAND (Russ. from 1809)   St Peters-burg

RUSSIAN EMPIRE

Union 1814–1905

K. OF NORWAY   K. OF SWEDEN

BALTIC SEA

K. OF DENMARK

NORTH SEA

K. OF PRUSSIA   Berlin   K. OF POLAND (united with Russia)   REP. OF KRAKOW

GREAT BRITAIN   London

K. OF THE NETHERLANDS   Lu.   O.   H.   Me.   S.

Paris   K. OF FRANCE   W.   B.   Pa.   K. OF BAVARIA   Vienna   AUSTRIAN EMPIRE

REP. OF SWITZERLAND   TYROL   ILLYRIA   LOMBARDY   K. OF P.   L.M.   T.   PAPAL STATES   Rome   OTTOMAN EMPIRE

Corsica   SARDINIA   K. OF THE TWO SICILIES   Ionian Is. (Br.)

K. OF PORTUGAL   Lisbon   K. OF SPAIN   Madrid   ANDORRA   Balearic Is.   MEDITERRANEAN SEA   Malta (Br.)

ALGERIA   TUNIS

88. SOUTH AMERICA 1810-1914

—— Boundary of Great Colombia 1819-30
Other boundaries as in 1914

0   500   1000 miles

ATLANTIC OCEAN

Caracas   VENEZUELA Spanish to 1811

Trinidad (Br.)   Georgetown   British   Cayenne   French   Suriname   Dutch   Guiana

COLOMBIA Spanish to 1811   Bogotá (NEW GRANADA Spanish to 1811)   GREAT COLOMBIA 1819-30

Quito   ECUADOR   Guayaquil

Pará   Amazon   Rio Negro   Tocantins   Pernambuco   Bahia

B R A Z I L
Portuguese colony to 1815
K. in union with Portugal 1815-22
Independent empire 1822-89
Republic from 1889

Trujillo   PERU Lima Spanish to 1821   Cuzco   Ayacucho   1821

BOLIVIA La Paz Spanish to 1825   Sucre   1825   Rio de Janeiro   Santos

PACIFIC OCEAN

PARA-GUAY   To Brazil 1821-28

Paraná   CHILE Spanish to 1810/18   Santiago   ARGENTINA Spanish to 1810/16   URUGUAY Spanish to 1814. To Brazil 1821-28   Montevideo   Buenos Aires

PATAGONIA to Argentina 1832

PANAMA Republic 1903

Falkland Is.

Tierra del Fuego

89.-90. UNIFICATION OF ITALY 1859-70

89. NORTHERN ITALY 1859

Dates show the year of incorporation into the Kingdom of Sardinia

0   25   50 miles

SWITZERLAND

TYROL

AUSTRIA

VENETIA

ISTRIA

Trieste

K. OF
Novara
PIEDMONT

LOMBARDY
Magenta 1859
Milan
Lodi
Solferino×
Pavia
Cremona
Piacenza

Lake
Maggiore
Lake
Como
Lake
Garda

Verona
×Custozza
Villafranca
Mantua

Padua
Venice

Adria

Alessandria

SARDINIA

D. OF PARMA
1860
Parma

Guastalla
(to Parma)
D. OF
MODENA
1860

ROMAGNA
1860

Ferrara

Rhône
Adige
Adda
Ticino
Po

90. THE KINGDOM OF SARDINIA

SWITZERLAND

AUSTRIAN EMPIRE

SAVOY
(Fr. 1860)

K. OF
Turin
PIEDMONT
SARDINIA
Genoa
5 May 1860

TYROL
LOMBARDY
Milan
Solferino

VENETIA
1866
Venice
Trieste
CROATIA

DALMATIA
Zara

TURKEY

FRENCH

NICE
(Fr. 1860)
MONACO
Nice

EMPIRE

D. OF
PARMA
D. OF
MODENA
ROMAGNA

PAPAL

Florence

G. D. OF
TUSCANY

THE MARCHES

STATES

UMBRIA

Elba

1870

Rome

Corsica

Caprera

Sardinia

Garibaldi

ADRIATIC SEA

PONTECORVO
Capua
BENEVENTO
Gaëta
Naples 7 Sept. 1860
Salerno

K. OF

THE

TWO

TYRRHENIAN
SEA

MEDITERRANEAN SEA

Palermo   Messina
20 Aug. 1860
Reggio

Marsala
11 May 1860
Sicily

SICILIES

90. THE KINGDOM OF SARDINIA

Sardinia 1859
Austria and Austrian territory 1859
Sardinia, Spring 1860

To Kingdom of Sardinia, Autumn 1860
Garibaldi's exp. against the Two Sicilies
Dates are given for the incorporation of Venetia and
the remaining Papal States into the K. of Italy

0   100   200   300 miles

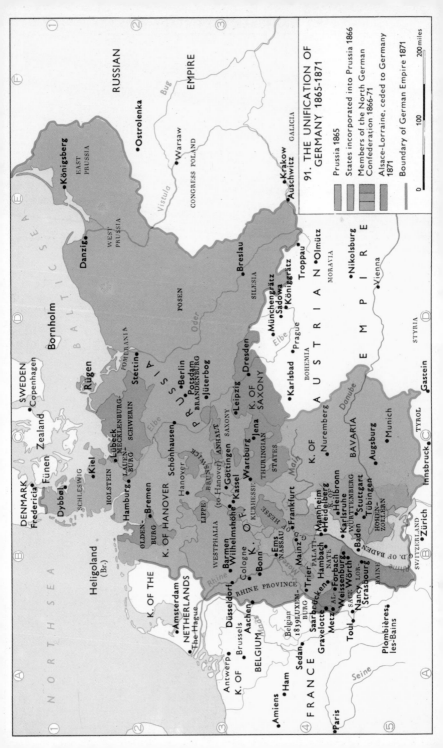

91. THE UNIFICATION OF GERMANY 1865-1871

Prussia 1865

States incorporated into Prussia 1866

Members of the North German Confederation 1866-71

Alsace-Lorraine, ceded to Germany 1871

Boundary of German Empire 1871

0   100   200 miles

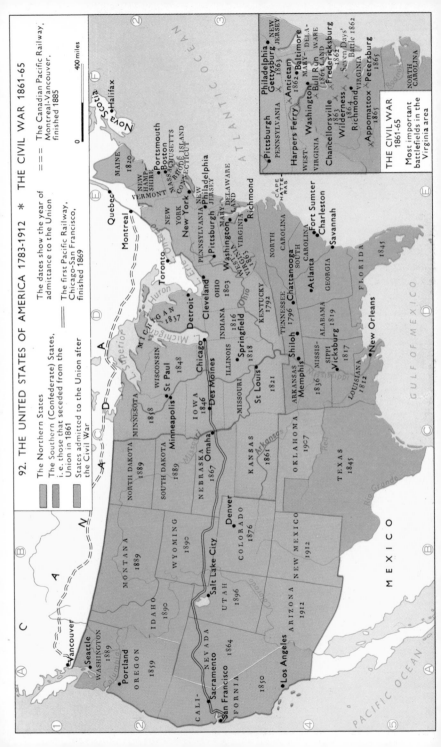

92. THE UNITED STATES OF AMERICA 1783-1912 * THE CIVIL WAR 1861-65

The Northern States

The Southern (Confederate) States, i.e. those that seceded from the Union in 1861

States admitted to the Union after the Civil War

The dates show the year of admittance to the Union

=== The first Pacific Railway, Chicago–San Francisco, finished 1869

=== The Canadian Pacific Railway, Montreal–Vancouver, finished 1885

0   400 miles

THE CIVIL WAR 1861-65
Most important battlefields in the Virginia area

PENNSYLVANIA
Pittsburgh • Philadelphia • Gettysburg 1863
WEST VIRGINIA
Harpers Ferry × Antietam 1862
Washington • Baltimore
MARY-LAND
DELA-WARE
× Bull Run 1861
Chancellorsville 1863
Wilderness × × Fredericksburg 1862 Seven Days' 1862
Richmond • 1865 × Battle 1862
VIRGINIA
Appomattox × × Petersburg 1865
NORTH CAROLINA

93. THE BALKANS AFTER THE CONGRESS OF BERLIN 1878

Turkish territory, occupied and administered by Austria-Hungary

Boundary of the large Bulgaria proposed by Russia in the preliminary treaty of San Stefano

0   100   200   300 miles

RUSSIA

BESSARABIA
Jassy
MOLDAVIA
CRIMEA
Eupatoria
Sevastopol • Alma
Inkerman
Balaklava
Romanian 1856-78

CROATIA
AUSTRIA-HUNGARY
WALLACHIA
Belgrade
Bucharest
ROMANIA
BOSNIA
SERBIA
Plevna
BULGARIA
(under Turkish suzerainty)
Sarajevo
HERZE-
GOVINA
MONTE-
NEGRO
Sofia
Shipka Pass
EAST RUMELIA
DALMATIA
ALBANIA
T
U
Adrianople
Constantinople
San Stefano • Scutari
Sea of Marmara
Gallipoli
Brussa
Salonika
R
K
E
Y
ITALY
ADRIATIC SEA
Ankara
Sinope
BLACK SEA

Ionian Is.
(to Greece 1865)
THESSALY
AEGEAN
SEA
Lesbos
Chios
Smyrna
GREECE • Athens
MOREA
Navarino•
Rhodes
Cyprus
(Br. 1878)

94. THE BALKANS AFTER THE WARS OF 1912-13

0   100   200   300 miles

RUSSIA

AUSTRIA-HUNGARY
TRANSYLVANIA
CRIMEA
Sevastopol
Drava
SLAVONIA
Sava
BANAT
ROMANIA
Bucharest
BOSNIA
(Annexed 1908)
Belgrade
Danube
DOBRUJA
Sarajevo
SERBIA
HERZEGOVINA
(Annexed 1908)
MONTE-
NEGRO
BULGARIA
Sofia
BLACK SEA
ALBANIA
Durazzo
MACEDONIA
Adrianople
Constantinople
THRACE
T
U
R
K
E
Y
Ankara
ITALY
ADRIATIC SEA
Salonika
Lemnos
Corfu
THESSALY
1881
AEGEAN
SEA
Lesbos
Chios
GREECE • Athens
MOREA
Dodecanese
(Ital. from 1912)
Rhodes
Cyprus
↓ Crete
(Greek 1908/12)

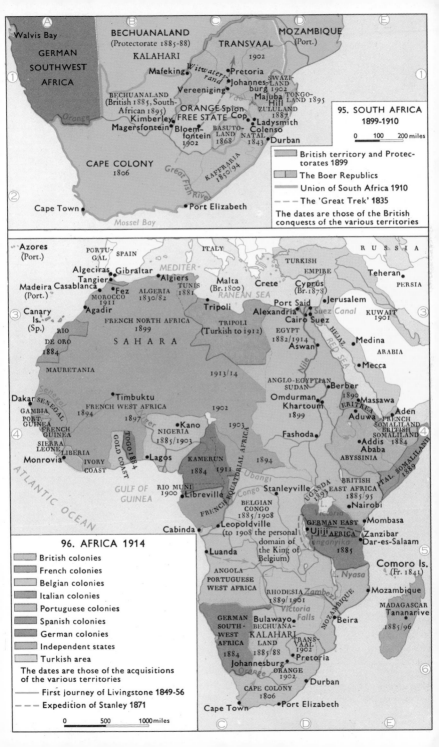

95. SOUTH AFRICA 1899-1910

0   100   200 miles

- British territory and Protectorates 1899
- The Boer Republics
- Union of South Africa 1910
- The 'Great Trek' 1835

The dates are those of the British conquests of the various territories

Map 95 labels:

Walvis Bay
GERMAN SOUTHWEST AFRICA
BECHUANALAND (Protectorate 1885-88)
KALAHARI
TRANSVAAL 1902
MOZAMBIQUE (Port.)
Mafeking
Witwatersrand
Pretoria
Johannesburg 1902
SWAZILAND 1887
BECHUANALAND (British 1885, South-African 1895)
Vereeniging
Majuba Hill
TONGOLAND 1895
ORANGE FREE STATE
Spion Cop
ZULULAND
Kimberley
Ladysmith
Magersfontein
Bloemfontein 1902
BASUTOLAND 1868
Colenso
NATAL 1843
Durban
CAPE COLONY 1806
KAFFRARIA 1850/94
Great Fish River
Orange
Cape Town
Port Elizabeth
Mossel Bay

96. AFRICA 1914

- British colonies
- French colonies
- Belgian colonies
- Italian colonies
- Portuguese colonies
- Spanish colonies
- German colonies
- Independent states
- Turkish area

The dates are those of the acquisitions of the various territories

— First journey of Livingstone 1849-56
--- Expedition of Stanley 1871

0   500   1000 miles

Map 96 labels:

Azores (Port.)
PORTUGAL
SPAIN
ITALY
RUSSIA
TURKISH EMPIRE
Teheran
PERSIA
Algeciras
Gibraltar
Tangier
Algiers
Malta (Br. 1800)
Crete
Cyprus (Br. 1878)
Madeira (Port.)
Casablanca
Fez
ALGERIA 1830/82
TUNIS 1881
MEDITERRANEAN SEA
Port Said
Jerusalem
MOROCCO 1911
Agadir
Tripoli
Alexandria
Cairo
Suez
Suez Canal
KUWAIT 1901
Canary Is. (Sp.)
FRENCH NORTH AFRICA 1899
TRIPOLI (Turkish to 1912)
EGYPT 1882/1914
Aswan
HEJAZ
Medina
ARABIA
RIO DE ORO 1884
SAHARA
Nile
RED SEA
Mecca
MAURETANIA
1913/14
ANGLO-EGYPTIAN SUDAN
Berber
Massawa
Aden
Dakar
Timbuktu
Omdurman
Khartoum 1899
ERITREA 1890
SENEGAL
FRENCH WEST AFRICA 1894
1897
1902
Kano
1903
Fashoda
Aduwa
FRENCH SOMALILAND
BRITISH SOMALILAND 1884
GAMBIA
PORT. GUINEA
FRENCH GUINEA
NIGERIA 1885/1903
Addis Ababa
ITAL. SOMALILAND 1889
SIERRA LEONE
LIBERIA
IVORY COAST
GOLD COAST 1884
TOGO 1884
Lagos
KAMERUN 1884 1911
1894
ABYSSINIA
Monrovia
GULF OF GUINEA
RIO MUNI 1900
Libreville
FRENCH EQUATORIAL AFRICA
Ubangi
Stanleyville
UGANDA 1893
BRITISH EAST AFRICA 1885/95
GERMAN EAST AFRICA 1885
Mombasa
ATLANTIC OCEAN
Congo
BELGIAN CONGO 1885/1908 (to 1908 the personal domain of the King of Belgium)
Leopoldville
Ujiji
L. Victoria
Nairobi
Zanzibar
Dar-es-Salaam
Cabinda
Luanda
Tanganyika
Comoro Is. (Fr. 1841)
ANGOLA PORTUGUESE WEST AFRICA
RHODESIA 1889/1901
L. Nyasa
Zambesi
Mozambique
MADAGASCAR Tananarive 1885/96
Victoria Falls
MOZAMBIQUE
Beira
GERMAN SOUTHWEST AFRICA 1884
Bulawayo
BECHUANALAND 1885/88
KALAHARI
TRANSVAAL 1902
Pretoria
Johannesburg
ORANGE 1902
Durban
Orange
CAPE COLONY 1806
Cape Town
Port Elizabeth

97. ASIA 1914

Russia 1800
Russian acquisitions 1800-78
Russian acquisitions 1878-1914
British territory
French territory
Japanese territory
American territory
Dutch territory

Russian sphere of interest
British sphere of interest
French sphere of interest
Japanese sphere of interest
German sphere of interest

The dates are those of the acquisitions of the various territories.
See also Maps 75 and 80

0 200 400 600 800 1000miles

Simbirsk
Tobolsk
Samara
Sverdlovsk
(Ekaterinburg)
Trans-Siberian railway. Finished 1904.

Constantinople

BLACK SEA

TURKEY

Astrakhan

MEDI-
TERRA-
NEAN SEA
Cyprus

Kars

Baku

CASPIAN SEA

ARAL SEA

L. Balkhash

Alexandria
Cairo
Beirut
Suez Canal

Russian
Sphere
1907

Teheran

WEST TURKESTAN
Khiva 1847/73

TURK-
MENISTAN
1881/86

Merv

Bokhara
Samarkand

Tashkent

SINKIAN

BOKHARA
PAMIR
1893

RED SEA

KUWAIT
1901

PERSIA

Kabul

AFGHANISTAN

KASHMIR
1846

ARABIA

British
Sphere
1907   1893

Kandahar
1890

Lahore
Amritsar

PUNJAB
1849

Mecca

PERSIAN GULF

OMAN
(under British protection)

Muscat

BALUCHISTAN
1876

Indus

Delhi
Meerut

Karachi

SIND

RAJPUTANA

Agra
Cawnpore

OUDH
1856

Lucknow

Benares

HIMALAYA
NEPAL

Ganges

ERITREA
FR.
SOMALILAND
Aden

HADRAMAUT

ARABIAN SEA

BRITISH

INDIA

Chanderna
(Fr.)

Diu
(Port.)
Damão
(Port.)
Bombay

BRITISH
SOMALILAND

ETHIOPIA

Socotra

Goa
(Port.)

NIZAM

Hyderabad

Yanaon

ITAL. SOMALILAND

MYSORE

Bangalore
Mahé
(Fr.)

Madras
Pondichéry (Fr.)
Karikal (Fr.)

CEYLON
Colombo

INDIAN

OCEAN

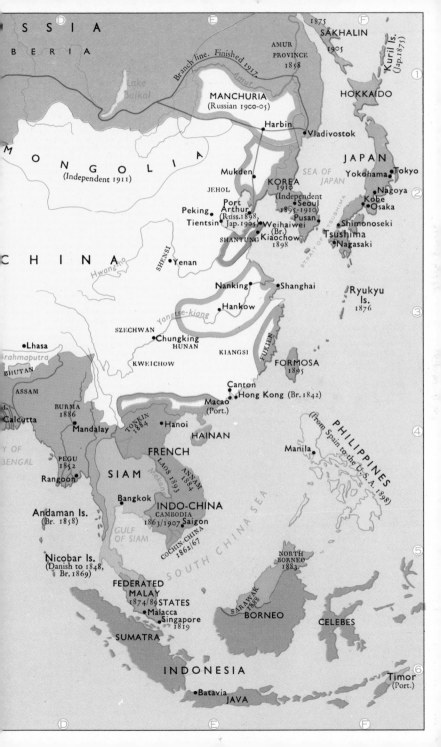

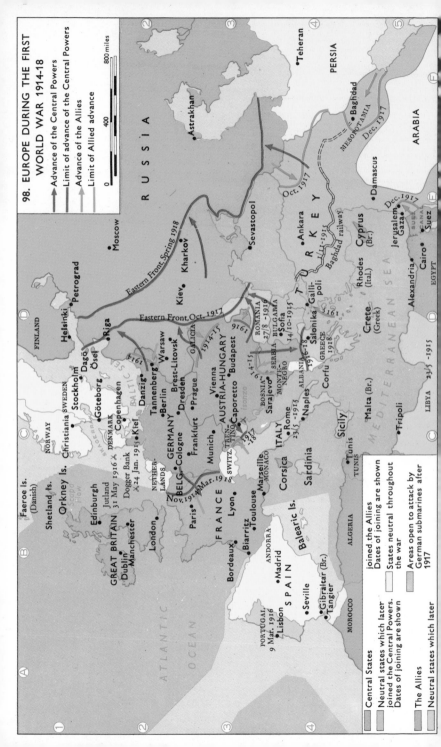

98. EUROPE DURING THE FIRST WORLD WAR 1914-18

Advance of the Central Powers
Limit of advance of the Central Powers
Advance of the Allies
Limit of Allied advance

0   400   800 miles

Central States

Neutral states which later joined the Central Powers. Dates of joining are shown

The Allies

Neutral states which later joined the Allies. Dates of joining are shown

States neutral throughout the war

Areas open to attack by German submarines after 1917

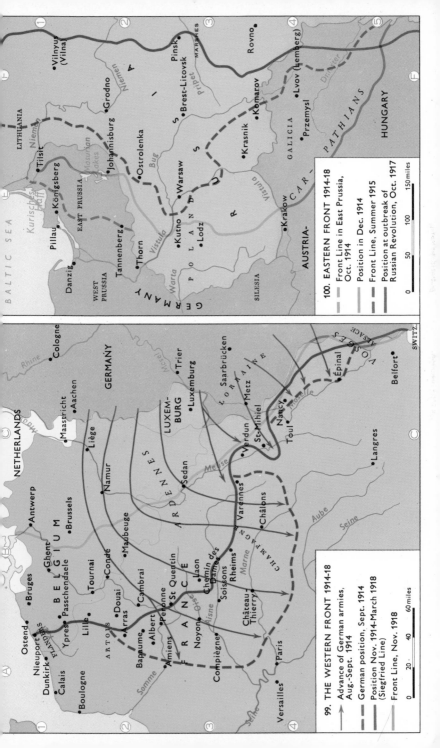

100. EASTERN FRONT 1914-18

- – – – Front Line in East Prussia, Oct. 1914
- ———— Position in Dec. 1914
- – – – Front Line, Summer 1915
- ———— Position at outbreak of Russian Revolution, Oct. 1917

0   50   100   150 miles

BALTIC SEA

Vilnyus (Vilna) • Grodno • Pinsk • Rovno •
Tilsit • Brest-Litovsk • Komarov • Lvov (Lemberg) •
Königsberg • Johannisburg • Ostrolenka • Krasnik • Przemysl •
Pillau • Danzig • EAST PRUSSIA • Tannenberg • Thorn • Warsaw • Kutno • Lodz •
WEST PRUSSIA • GERMANY • Kraków •
SILESIA • AUSTRIA- • HUNGARY

LITHUANIA
Niemen
Kurisches Haff
Masurian Lakes
PRIPET MARSHES
Bug
Vistula
POLAND
Warta
RUSSIA
GALICIA
CARPATHIANS
Dniester

99. THE WESTERN FRONT 1914-18

- ⟶ Advance of German armies, Aug.-Sept. 1914
- ———— German position, Sept. 1914
- ———— Position Nov. 1914-March 1918 (Siegfried Line)
- ———— Front Line, Nov. 1918

0   20   40   60 miles

NETHERLANDS

Cologne •
Maastricht • Aachen • Liège • Namur •
Ostend • Bruges • Ghent • Antwerp • Brussels •
Nieuport • Passchendaele • GERMANY • Trier •
Dunkirk • Ypres • Lille • Tournai • Maubeuge • LUXEM-BURG • Luxemburg •
Calais • FLANDERS • Condé • Cambrai • Sedan • Saarbrücken •
Boulogne • ARTOIS • Douai • ARDENNES • Metz •
Arras • St Quentin • Laon • Verdun • St Mihiel •
Bapaume • Péronne • Chemin des Dames • Varennes • Nancy •
Albert • Noyon • Soissons • Rheims • Châlons • Toul •
Amiens • Compiègne • FRANCE • Château Thierry • Langres • Épinal •
Paris • Versailles • Belfort •
SWITZ.

Rhine
Meuse
Moselle
Oise
Aisne
Somme
Marne
Seine
Aube
Moselle
LORRAINE
ALSACE
VOSGES
CHAMPAGNE

101. EUROPE 1919-35

— Boundaries of 1914

0 · · · 250 · · · 500 miles

102. CONQUESTS OF HITLER, MUSSOLINI AND FRANCO

GERMANY
At Hitler's accession to power 1933
Rhineland. Remilitarized 1936
Austria. Incorporated Mar. 1938 and named Ostmark
Sudetenland. Incorporated Oct. 1938
Bohemia, Moravia, Memel. Incorp. Mar. 1939
Slovakia. German controlled from 1939
Germany, Mar. 1939

ITALY
Albania. Italian, 1939
Ethiopian campaign, Oct. 1935
Ethiopia. Italian, May 1936

SPAIN
Areas supporting Franco at the outbreak of the Civil War, July 1936
Conquered area to Mar. 1937
Conquered area Mar. 1937-Dec. 1938
Conquered Dec. 1938-Mar. 1939
German and Italian support for Franco

103. EUROPE DURING THE SECOND WORLD WAR, SEPT. 1939–JUNE 1941

Western Powers at out-break of war 3 Sept. 1939

Germany, Sept. 1939

Italy at war with Western Powers, June 1940, and Bulgaria at war with Great Britain, Mar. 1941

Soviet Union, non-agres-sion pact with Germany from Aug. 1939–June 1941

Neutral countries, Sept. 1939

→ Axis advances to June 1941

→ Russian advances to June 1940

Russian boundary, June 1940

Occupied area of France after 26 June 1940

The light red boundaries show the political situation in Sept. 1939. Dates indicate time of German occupation

0   200   400   600 miles

ICELAND

Petsamo
Murmansk
Narvik
Salla
(occupied by Britain 1940)
Faeroe Is.
Suomussalmi
Namsos
FINLAND
Åndalsnes
Steinkjer
War with Russia
Nov. 1939–
Mar. 1940
Trondhjem
NORWAY
1940
Elverum
Viborg
Bergen
Hamar
SWEDEN
Helsinki
Lenin-grad
Stavanger
Oslo
June 1940
Stockholm
ESTONIA
June 1940
Christiansand
DENMARK
LATVIA
June 1940
GREAT
1940
LITHUANIA
EIRE
Dublin
Danzig
Minsk
Liverpool
BRITAIN
Berlin
Sept. 1939
Coventry
NETHER-
Warsaw
London
LANDS
POLAND
Dunkirk
BELGIUM
Kiev
Rouen
LUXEM-
Prague
Sept. 1939
1940
BURG
1939
NORTH
Sept. 1939
Paris
GERMANY
SLOVAKIA
BUKOVINA
FRANCE
Munich
June
Vichy
Bern Vienna
1940
BESSARABIA
SWITZ.
HUNGARY
Bordeaux
Milan
ROMANIA
Toulouse
PORTU-
Marseille
Belgrade
Bucharest
GAL
Lisbon
Madrid
YUGOSLAVIA
SOUTH DOBRUJA
(Bulg. Sept. 1940)
SPAIN
Corsica
Rome
Sofia
BUL-
GARIA
Sardinia
1941
ITALY
T
Naples
U
Ankara
Gibraltar (Br.)
R
sp.Tangier
ALBANIA
K
E
Y
PERSIA
MOROCCO
(It.)
GREECE
MOROCCO
ALGERIA
TUNISIA
Sicily
1941
Athens
SYRIA
(Fr.)
(Fr.)
(Fr.)
Malta
Crete
Cyprus
(Fr. mandate)
IRAQ
(Br.)

104. EUROPE DURING THE SECOND WORLD WAR, OCT. 1942–MAY 1945

0   400   800 miles

Germany and its allies 1942

Area under German and Ital. control Oct. 1942

Area under Allied control Oct. 1942

Neutral countries 1942

FINLAND
armistice
4 Sept. 1944
Viborg
June
1944
SWEDEN
Helsinki
Leningrad
GREAT
Edinburgh
DENMARK
Riga
EIRE
Moscow
BRITAIN
Copenhagen
Vilnyus
Katyn
SOVIET
Hamburg
Danzig
Smolensk
Voronesh
London
NETHER-
Lübeck
Minsk
LANDS
Bergen-Belsen
Berlin
Arnhem
Warsaw
UNION
Contentin
BELGIUM
Torgau
Brest-Litovsk
BRITANY
Caen
Cologne
Buchenwald
Stalingrad
Falaise
Remagen
Schweinfurt
Prague
Auschwitz
Kiev
Kharkov
Argentan
Paris
Pilsen
Lvov
Aug. 1944
Dachau
SLOVAKIA
Nuremberg
Stalino
Vichy
Munich
Vienna
SWITZ.
Berchtes-
Budapest
Bordeaux
Lyon
gaden
HUNGARY
Crimea
Milan
Yalta
ROMANIA
CAUCASUS
Corsica
Belgrade
YUGOSLAVIA
PORTUGAL
Madrid
BULGARIA
SPAIN
Rome
Sofia
Istanbul
Sardinia
Sept.
1943
Naples
Ankara
TURKEY
Amer. and
Brit. troops
Nov. 1942
Oran
Algiers
Sicily
MOROCCO
Tunis
July 1943
GREECE
British troops
SYRIA
ALGERIA
May 1943
Malta
Crete
Cyprus
PALE-
STINE
IRAQ
British troops
Tripoli
Jan. 1943
Tobruk
JORDAN
Benghazi
El Alamein
Alexandria
LIBYA
Nov. 1942
EGYPT
ARABIA

Front lines May 1944

Front lines Dec. 1944

→ Allied advances

Black boundaries show the political situation in September 1939

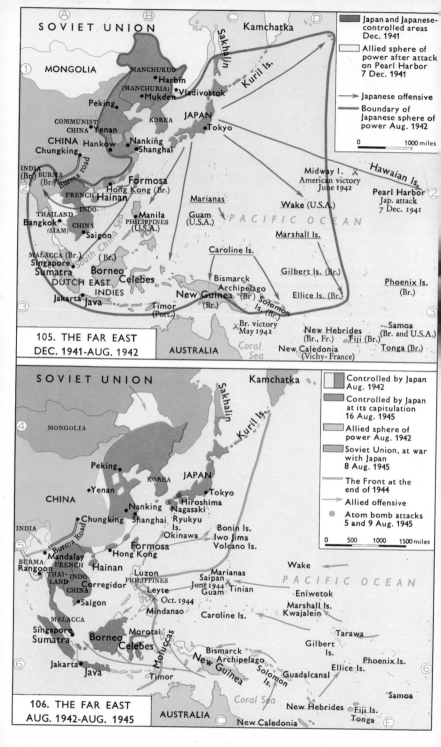

Map 105

105. THE FAR EAST DEC. 1941–AUG. 1942

Legend:
- Japan and Japanese-controlled areas Dec. 1941
- Allied sphere of power after attack on Pearl Harbor 7 Dec. 1941
- Japanese offensive
- Boundary of Japanese sphere of power Aug. 1942

0 — 1000 miles

SOVIET UNION

MONGOLIA

Kamchatka

Sakhalin

Kuril Is.

MANCHUKUO (MANCHURIA)
Harbin
Vladivostok
Mukden

Peking

KOREA

JAPAN
Tokyo

COMMUNIST CHINA
Yenan

CHINA
Hankow
Nanking
Shanghai

Chungking

INDIA (Br.)
BURMA (Br.)
Burma road

Formosa

Hong Kong (Br.)

FRENCH
Hainan

THAILAND (SIAM)
Bangkok
INDO-CHINA
Manila
PHILIPPINES (U.S.A.)
Saigon

Guam (U.S.A.)

Marianas

Wake (U.S.A.)

Midway I. ✗
American victory June 1942

Hawaian Is.

Pearl Harbor
Jap. attack 7 Dec. 1941

PACIFIC OCEAN

MALACCA (Br.)
Singapore
Sumatra
Borneo (Br.)
DUTCH EAST INDIES
Celebes

South China Sea

Marshall Is.

Caroline Is.

Gilbert Is. (Br.)

Phoenix Is. (Br.)

Jakarta Java

Timor (Port.)

New Guinea (Br.)

Bismarck Archipelago (Br.)

Solomon Is. (Br.)

Ellice Is. (Br.)

Br. victory ✗ May 1942

New Hebrides (Br., Fr.)
Fiji (Br.)

Samoa (Br. and U.S.A.)

Tonga (Br.)

AUSTRALIA

Coral Sea

New Caledonia (Vichy-France)

Map 106

106. THE FAR EAST AUG. 1942–AUG. 1945

Legend:
- Controlled by Japan Aug. 1942
- Controlled by Japan at its capitulation 16 Aug. 1945
- Allied sphere of power Aug. 1942
- Soviet Union, at war with Japan 8 Aug. 1945
- The Front at the end of 1944
- Allied offensive
- Atom bomb attacks 5 and 9 Aug. 1945

0 — 500 — 1000 — 1500 miles

SOVIET UNION

MONGOLIA

Kamchatka

Sakhalin

Kuril Is.

Peking

KOREA

JAPAN
Tokyo

Yenan

CHINA
Nanking
Shanghai

Chungking

Hiroshima
Nagasaki
Ryukyu Is.
Okinawa

INDIA

Burma Road

Bonin Is.
Iwo Jima
Volcano Is.

BURMA
Mandalay
Rangoon
FRENCH
THAI-LAND
INDO-CHINA
Corregidor
Saigon

Formosa

Hong Kong

Hainan

Luzon
PHILIPPINES
Leyte
Oct. 1944
Mindanao

Wake

Marianas
Saipan
June 1944 ✗
Guam Tinian

Eniwetok

PACIFIC OCEAN

Caroline Is.

Marshall Is.
Kwajalein

Tarawa

MALACCA
Singapore
Sumatra

Borneo
Celebes
Moluccas

Morotai

Gilbert Is.

Phoenix Is.

Jakarta Java

Timor

Bismarck Archipelago

New Guinea

Solomon Is.

Guadalcanal

Ellice Is.

Samoa

Coral Sea

New Hebrides
Fiji Is.
Tonga

AUSTRALIA

New Caledonia

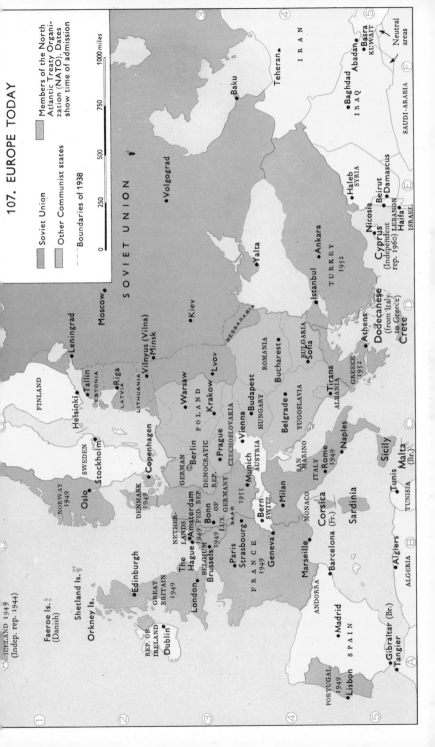

107. EUROPE TODAY

Members of the North Atlantic Treaty Organization (NATO). Dates show time of admission

Soviet Union

Other Communist states

– – – Boundaries of 1938

0   250   500   750   1000 miles

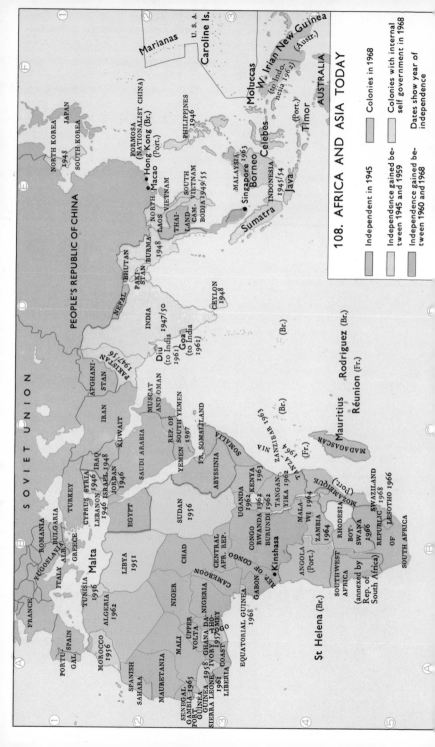

108. AFRICA AND ASIA TODAY

Independent in 1945

Independence gained between 1945 and 1959

Independence gained between 1960 and 1968

Colonies in 1968

Colonies with internal self government in 1968

Dates show year of independence

INDEX

The index contains all the place names on the maps, and also names of peoples (e.g. Goths), historical events (e.g. Civil War in England), military expeditions (e.g. Marlborough), voyages of discovery (e.g. Columbus), etc.

Towns and cities which appear on more than one map are generally given a reference to only one map—the one on which they are most important historically, or, for very common names, the one on which they can be most easily found, i.e. generally the map drawn to the largest scale.

More than one reference is given to places important at different times for different reasons. Poitiers, for example, has a reference to Map 33—the battle between Charles Martel and the Moslems in 732—and to Map 43, where it is shown as important in the civilization of medieval Europe.

Countries, provinces, regions, etc.—the boundaries of which may alter with time—are given several references in chronological order, so that their development may be traced. Bulgaria, for example, has sixteen references for the period 900 to 1968; and if one is interested in the political situation in Italy at the beginning of the eighteenth century there are references to two maps, showing the situation in 1701 and 1721.

For references to wide historical periods or concepts which cannot be immediately found in the index, the list of contents at the beginning of the book should be consulted.

The italic number is the number of the map; the letter and number which follow show the area on the map in which the name will be found. (It is to be supposed that each map is divided into squares by lines drawn down the page midway between the letters and across the page midway between the numbers.)

Names in parentheses are alternative names or spellings; those preceded by *mod.* are the modern or present-day names of the localities. Classical names of towns and cities are given in their Latin form.

Alessandria *89*A2
Alet *49*B5
Alexander the Great
    Empire of *22*
    route of, 334–323 B.C. *22*
Alexandria (*mod.* Iskenderun)
    Asia Minor *22*B2
Alexandria, Babylonia *22*D4
Alexandria, Bactria *22*F2
Alexandria, Carmania *22*E4
Alexandria, Egypt *22*B3
Alexandria, Gedrosia *22*F4
Alexandria (*mod.* Ghazni) *22*F3
Alexandria (*mod.* Herat) *22*E3
Alexandria, India Inferior *22*F4
Alexandria (*mod.* Kandahar) *22*F3
Alexandria Eschata *22*F1
Alexandria Margiane (*mod.* Merv)
    *22*E2
Alexandria Sogdiana *22*F3
Alexandropolis *22*E2
Algarve *55*A6
Algeciras *96*B3
Algeria, 1812 *86*B5
    1914 *96*B3   1914–18 *98*B5
    1919–35 *101*A2   1939–41 *103*A3
    1942–45 *104*A-B6
    1968 *107*B5, *108*A1–2
Algiers, 1556 *57*B6
Algiers (town) *107*B5
Algonkin *59*D3
Alicante *39*B6
Alkmaar *61*C2
Allegheny Mts. *78*E3
Allen, route of, 1885 *59*B1
Allier (river) *69*E3–4
Allies, during First
    World War *98*
Alma *93*E1
Almaden *46*A6
Almagro *see* Pizarro
Almanza *76*B6
Almendralejo *32*A4
Almeria *55*C6
Al Mina (Posidion) *11*F3
Almissa *49*E5
Almoravides, Dominions of the
    1100 *39*B6
Alpes Montes (the Alps)
    *27*F3–4
Alpheus (river) *14*B3
Alsace
    936 *38*B2–3   *c.* 1630 *64*B6
    1914–18 *99*D5   1919–35 *101*B2
Alsace-Lorraine, 1871 *91*B4–5
Alstahaug *70*B1
Altamaha (river) *78*D-E4
Altamira *1*A2
Altdorf *48*C5
Althing *37*A1
Altmark (town) *70*C5
Altmark, Brandenburg, 1415 *81*C3
Altranstadt *73*B2
Amalfi *39*D5
Amanus, Mt. *6*C2
Amasia *26*C1

Amazon (river) *88*E-F2
Ambarri *27*F3
Amboise *62*C3
Ambracia *20*B2
Ameland *61*D1
Amenophis II
    Mortuary temple of *5*
Amenophis II
    Temple of *4*
Amenophis III
    Mortuary temple of *5*
American Indians *59*
Amiens *43*C2, *51*C3
Amisus (*mod.* Samsun) *26*C1
Amiternum
    (*mod.* San Vittorino) *25*E2
Amman *41*C6
Ammon, 800 B.C. *9*F4
Amon, Oracle of *10*A4
Amon, Temple of, Karnak *4*
Amorgos *14*E3
Amphipolis *14*C1
Amq *6*C2
Amritsar *97*C3
Amsterdam *61*D2
Amur (river) *42*E1
Amur Province, 1914 *97*E-F1
Anapus (river) *16*C3
Anas (*mod.* Guadiana, river) *25*A3–4
Anatolia *53*D5
Ancona *35*E2, *45*E3
Ancyra (*mod.* Ankara) *22*B2, *26*C2
Åndalsnes *103*B1
Andalusia *55*B6
Andaman Is.
    1858 *80*F4   1914 *97*D5
Andorra
    1812 *86*B4   1815 *87*B4
    1914–18 *98*B3   1968 *107*B4
Andros *14*D3, *15*E6
Andrussov *72*B4
Ångermanland *70*C2
Angers *43*B3
Anghiari *45*D3
Angles *32*C1
Anglicans in Europe, 1560 *63*
Anglo-Egyptian Sudan, 1914 *96*D4
Anglo-Saxon kingdoms *32*B1–2
Angola
    1750 *75*D4   1914 *96*C5
    1968 *108*B4
Angora (*mod.* Ankara) *42*A2, *52*D2
Angoulême (province) *50*B6
Angoulême (town) *36*B5, *43*B3
Angoumois *69*D4
Angus *65*D2
Anhalt
    1648 *67*C3   1871 *91*C3
Anibe *2*A4
Anjou
    1100 *39*B3   1180–1453 *50*
    1429 *51*B4   1562–92 *62*B3
Ankara *93*E2
Anna, Empress of Russia
    expansion under, 1730–40 *72*
Annam, 1914 *97*E4

B

Brabant
  1429 *51*E3
  1579 *61*C-D3–4
Bradford *65*D3
Braga *55*A5
Brahestad *70*D2
Brahmaputra (river) *80*F2
Brandenburg (town) *44*C4
Brandenburg-Prussia
  1415–1797 *81*   *c.* 1630 *64*D4
  1648 *67*C-D2   1700 *73*B2
  1701 *71*D1–2   1721 *76*D3
Bratislava (Pressburg) *71*E3
Brazil
  c. 1600 *58*B4   1750 *75*B-C4
  1815–1914 *88*E-F1–4
Breda *61*C3
Breida Fjord *37*A1
Breisach *69*F2
Breisgau, 1648 *67*B5
Breitenfeld *64*D5
Bremen *38*B1, *43*C1, *44*B4, *67*C2
Bremen, Archbishopric of
  c. 1630 *64*C4
  1648 *67*C2
Brenner Pass *38*C3
Brescia *45*C1
Breslau *44*D5, *82*E3
Brest-Litovsk *100*F3
Brétigny *51*C4
Bretland (Wales) *37*B2
Briel *61*C3
Brienne *86*C3
Brihuega *102*B5
Brindisi *38*E5
Bristol *65*D4
Britannia *28*B1
Britannia Inferior, A.D. 117 *29*B1
Britannia Minor (Brittany) *32*B2
Britannia Superior, A.D. 117 *29*A1
British colonies, 1750 *75*
British East Africa, 1914 *96*E4–5
British Guiana (*mod.* Guyana)
  1914 *88*E1
British India, 1914 *97*B-D3–5
  See also India
British (Celtic) kingdoms
  526 *32*A-B1–2
British Somaliland
  1914 *96*E4, *97*A4
Brittany (Britannia Minor) *32*B2
  814 *33*A3   843 *36*A4
  c. 900 *37*B3   1100 *39*B3
  1180–1453 *50*   1429 *51*A4
Brixen *49*D4
Brixen, Bishopric of, 1648 *67*C6
Brno (Brünn) *86*D3
Bromley, London *66*E6
Brompton, London *66*A6
Brömsebro *70*B4
Bruges *44*A5, *61*B3
Brule, route of *59*C3
Brundisium (*mod.* Brindisi) *23*E2
Brunete *102*A5
Brünn (Brno) *86*D3

Brunswick *44*C4
Brunswick, Duchy of, 1871 *91*C3
Brussa *60*C3
Brussels *43*C2, *61*C4
Bruttium *23*D3
Bucephala *22*F3
Bucharest *60*C2, *76*F4, *93*C1
Buchenwald *104*C5
Buckingham *65*D4
Buckingham Palace, London *66*B6
Buda *39*E4, *43*D3, *60*B1
Budapest *98*C4, *104*C5, *107*C4
Buenaventura *56*D2
Buenos Aires (province) *88*E4
Buenos Aires (town) *88*E4
Bug (river running into Black Sea)
  *74*C-D6
Bug (tributary of the Vistula)
  *74*B5
Bulawayo *96*D6
Bulgar *42*B1
Bulgaria, *c.* 900 *37*D4
  1230 *40*D-E2–3
  1265 *52*B1   1355 *53*B4
  1453 *60*C2   1556 *57*E3
  1701 *71*F4   1721 *76*F4
  1812 *86*E4   1878 *93*B-C2
  1912–13 *94*C5   1914–18 *98*D4
  1919–35 *101*C2
  1939–41 *103*C3
  1942–45 *104*D5
  1968 *107*D4
Bulgars
  526 *32*D-E4   814 *33*C3
Bull Run *92*F4
Bunzelwitz *82*E3
Burdigala (*mod.* Bordeaux) *27*D4
Burgos *39*B4, *43*B4, *49*A5
Burgundian kingdom, 526 *32*B3
Burgundian migrations *32*
Burgundy, Domains of, 1429 *51*
Burgundy, Duchy of, 1100 *39*C3–4
  1180–1453 *50*   1429 *51*D5
  16th century *62*D3
Burgundy, Kingdom of, 1100 *39*C4
Burgundy, Lower, *c.* 900 *37*B4
Burgundy, Upper, *c.* 900 *37*C4
Burkersdorf *82*E3
Burma
  1914 *97*D4
  1941–42 *105*A2
  1942–45 *106*A5
  1968 *108*D-E2
Burma Road *106*A5
Burundi *108*B4
Bury St Edmunds *43*B1
Byblos
  1400 B.C. *6*C2   860 B.C. *9*E1
Byzantine Empire
  526 *32*D-F4–5   814 *33*B-D3–4
  c. 900 *37*C-E5   1100 *39*E-F5–6
  1256 *52*   1355 *53*
Byzantine territories, 1100 *40*
Byzantium (*mod.* Istanbul)
  *21*F1, *28*E3

D

E

G

Gabon *108*B3–4
Gades (*mod*. Cadiz) *25*A4
Gaeta *90*C4
Gaetulia *25*C5
Gainsborough *65*E3
Galapagos Is. *56*B3
Galatia, 189 B.C. *26*B-C2
   44 B.C. *28*E3   A.D. 117 *29*D3
Galicia, Spain *55*A4
Galicia, Poland
   1701 *71*E-F2   1756–63 *82*F4
   1772 *84*D4   1812 *86*D-E3
   1914–18 *98*D3, *100*E-F4
Galilee *41*B5
Galilee, Sea of *9*E2–3
Gallia Belgica *27*E-F1
Gallia Celtica *27*D-F2–4
Gallia Cisalpina *25*D-E1
Gallia Cispadana *23*B1
Gallia Narbonensis *27*E-F4
Gallia Transalpina *25*C-D2
Gallia Transpadana *23*A1
Gallipoli *60*C3, *98*D4
Galveston *59*B4
Gama, Vasco da, route of
   1498 *58*C4–5, and D-E4
Gambia, 1750 *75*C3
   1914 *96*A4   1968 *108*A3
Ganges (river) *80*E-F2
Gangra *26*C1
Gap *49*C5
Garda, Lake *45*C1
Garibaldi, expedition against
   the Kingdom of the
   Two Sicilies, 1860 *90*
Garigliano (river) *45*E4
Garonne (river) *51*C6
Garumna (*mod*. Garonne, river)
   *27*D-E4
Gascony, 1100 *39*B4
   1429 *51*B6   1562–92 *62*B4
Gastein *91*C5
Gath *9*D4
Gaugamela *22*C2
Gaul *27*
Gävle *70*C3
Gaza *22*B3
Gedrosia (Baluchistan) *22*E4
Gela *16*B3
Gelas (river) *16*C3
Gelderland, 1579 *61*D-E2
Gelderland, Upper
   1579 *61*D-E3   1715 *81*A3
Gelnhausen *39*C3
Gembloux *61*C4
Genava (*mod*. Geneva) *27*F3
Generality, The, 1648 *68*B-C3–4
Geneva *48*A6
Geneva, Lake of *48*A6
Genghis Khan, Empire of, 1227 *42*
   most important campaigns *42*
Genoa *45*B2
Genoa, Republic of, 1454 *45*A2
   1556 *57*C3–4
   1721 *76*C-D4–5

Genoese settlements in Aegean Sea
   and on Black Sea coast, 1355 *53*
Genseric *32*C5
Genua (*mod*. Genoa) *23*A1
Georgetown *88*E1
Georgia, Asia *60*E3
Georgia, U.S.A., 1763 *77*B4
   1783 *78*D4   1861–65 *92*D4
Gepides, Kingdom of the, 526 *32*D3
Gergovia *27*E3
Gerizim, Mt. *9*E3, *41*B5
German Confederation, 1815 *87*
German Democratic Republic
   1968 *107*B-C3
German East Africa (Tanganyika)
   1914 *96*D-E5
German Empire, 1701 *71*C-E1–3
   1721 *76*   1871 *91*
   See also Germany
Germania, A.D. 117 *29*B-C1–2
Germania Inferior, A.D. 117 *29*B1
Germania Magna *28*C-D1
Germania Superior, A.D. 117 *29*B2
German South-West Africa
   c. 1900 *95*A1   1914 *96*C6
Germany
   526 *32*C-D2–3   843 *36*C-E4–5
   c. 900 *37*C3   936 *38*A-D1–3
   1100 *39*C-D2–4
   1230 *40*B-C1–2
   1370 (North Germany) *44*B-D4–5
   1378–1417 *47*C-E2
   1556 *57*C-D1–3
   during Thirty Year's War
   1618–48 *64*
   1648 *67*
   1701 *71*C-D1–3
   1721 *76*C-D3–4
   during Seven Year's War,
   1756–63 *82*
   1812 *86*C-D2–3
   1815 *87*B-C2–3
   1865–71
   (unification of Germany) *91*
   1914–18 *98*C2–3
   1919–35 *101*B-C1–2
   1936–39 *102*
   1939–41 *103*B-C2
   1942–45 *104*B-C4–5
   1968 *107*B3
Germany, Federal Republic of
   *107*B3
Gettysburg *92*F4
Ghana, 1968 *108*A3
   See also Gold Coast
Ghent *61*B4, *99*B1
Gibraltar (Jebel Tarik)
   *33*A4, *55*B6, *76*B6, *98*B4, *107*A5
Gien *62*C3
Gilbert Is. *105*D3, *106*D6
Gilboa, Mt. *9*E3, *41*B5
Giza *2*A1, *3*
Glandève *49*C5
Glarus *48*D5
Glasgow *43*B1, *65*C2

H

Hadria *11*C1
Hadrianopolis *29*D3
Hadrumetum (*mod.* Sousse) *25*E5
Hague, The *61*C2, *107*B3
Haguenau *67*B4, *69*F2
Haifa *107*E5
Hainan, 1914 *97*E4
    1941–42 *105*A2
    1942–45 *106*A5
Hainault, 1579 *61*B-C4
Haiti *56*D-E1
    1650–1763 *77*   1750 *75*B3
Halberstadt *49*D2
Halberstadt, Bishopric of
    1648 *67*C3, *81*C3
    1756–63 *82*C3
Haleb (Aleppo) *6*C2, *107*E5
Haliacmon (river) *14*B1
Halicarnassus *20*D4
Halifax, Nova Scotia *59*E3, *78*F1
Halland, 1660 *70*B4
Halle *44*C5, *67*C4, *82*C3
Halles, Les, Paris *83*B2
Halupe *8*A1
Halycus (river) *16*B3
Halys (river) *10*B2
Ham *91*A4
Hama *41*C3
Hamadan *33*E3, *42*B3
Hamar *103*C1
Hambach *86*C3
Hamburg *44*C4
Hameln *44*B5
Hampshire *51*B-C3
Hangchow *42*F3
Hangö (Gangud) *70*D3
Hankow *97*E3, *105*B2
Hannibal
    expedition of, 220–203 B.C. *25*
Hanoi *97*E4
Hanover (town) *44*C4, *82*C2
Hanover
    1701 *71*D1–2   1721 *76*D3
    1756–63 *82*B-C2
    1815 *87*B-O2
    1866 *91*B-C2–3
Hanse towns *44*
Hanseatic League *44*
Hanseatic trading depots and
    settlements *44*
Harbin *97*E1
Harfleur *51*C3
Härje Valley, 1660 *70*B2
Härnösand *70*C2
Harpers Ferry *92*F4
Harwich *65*E4
Harzburg *38*C1
Hasdrubal
    expedition of, 208–207 B.C. *25*
Hastenbeck *82*C2
Hastings *39*B3
Hatfield *65*E4
Hatshepsut, tomb of *5*
Hattushash (*mod.* Bogaz-Köy) *6*B1
Havana *56*C1, *58*A3, *59*C4
Havel (river) *81*C-D2–3

Havelberg *49*D1
Hawaiian Is. *105*E2
Hazor *9*E2
Hebron *41*B6
Hecatompylus *22*D2
Hedemora *70*B3
Heidaby *37*C2
Heidelberg *43*C2, *91*B4
Heilbronn *67*C4
Hejaz *33*D4
Helena *59*B3
Helicon, Mt. *15*B5
Heligoland *36*C4, *91*B1
Heliopolis *2*A1
Helios, chariot of, Delphi *19*C4
Hellespont *14*E1
Helluland *58*B2
Helsingfors (*mod.* Helsinki) *86*D1
Helsingland *70*B-C2
Helsinki (Helsingfors) *98*D1
Helvetian Republic
    1800 *85*A-B1   1812 *86*C3
Helwan *2*A2
Hera, Temple of, Olympia *18*B1
Heraclea *41*A1
Heraclea (*mod.* Eregli)
    Bithynia *26*B1
Heraclea (*mod.* Sevastopol)
    Crimea *11*E1
Heraclea, Lucania *21*B2, *23*D3
Heraclea Minoa, Sicily *16*A3
Heracleopolis *2*A2
Heracleum
    (*mod.* Candia, Iraklion) *12*C
Herat *22*E3, *42*B3
Herculaneum *23*C2
Hercules, Pillars of *25*A5
Hereford (county) *51*B2
Hereford (town) *49*B1
Hermannstadt *60*C2
Hermonthis *2*B3
Hermopolis *2*A2
Hermus (river) *20*D-E3
Herodes, Odeum of, Acropolis
    Athens *17*B5
Hersfeld *43*C2
Hertford *51*C2
Hertogenbosch *68*C3
Herzegovina, 1556 *57*D4
    1878 *93*A2   1912–13 *94*A5
Hesse
    936 *38*B2   c. 1630 *64*C5
Hesse, Grand Duchy of, 1871 *91*B4
Hesse-Darmstadt, Landgraviate of
    1648 *67*C3
Hesse-Kassel, Landgraviate of
    1648 *67*C3
Hibernia *29*A1
Hieraconpolis *2*B3
Hierosolyma (Jerusalem) *28*F4
Hildesheim *38*C1
Hildesheim, Bishopric of
    1648 *67*C3
Himalayas *80*E-F1–2
Himera (river) *16*B3
Himera (town) *16*B2

I

J

Japan, Sea of *97*F2
Jarnac *62*B4
Jarrow *43*B1
Jassy *93*C1
Java *1*F5
   c. 1600 *58*E-F4   1750 *75*E4
   1914 *97*E6   1968 *108*E4
Jaxartes (river) *22*E1
Jebel Tarik (Gibraltar) *33*A4
Jehol, 1914 *97*E2
Jellinge *37*C2
Jena *86*C3
Jerez de la Frontera *33*A4
Jericho *9*E4
Jerusalem, 1400 B.C. *6*B3
   860 B.C. *9*E4   1140 *41*B6
Jerusalem, Kingdom of
   *41*B4–6
Jervaulx *43*B1
Joan of Arc, campaign of *51*
Jodhpur *80*D2
Johannesburg *95*C1

Johannisburg *100*E2
Jomsborg *38*D1
Jönköping *70*B4
Joppa (Jaffa) *9*D4
Jordan (river) *9*E3–4
Jordan (state)
   1942–45 *104*E6
   1968 *108*B-C2
Judah, 860 B.C. *9*D-E5
Jugurtha, Kingdom of *25*
Jülich *61*E4
Jülich, County of, 1648 *67*B3
Julius Caesar, Temple of
   Rome *31*C6(7)
Jumna (river) *80*E2
Juno Moneta, Temple of
   Rome *31*A5
Jupiter, Temple of, Rome *31*A6
Jüterbog *91*C3
Jutland *44*C3
Jutland, Battle of
   31 May 1916 *98*C2

K

Kabelvåg *70*C1
Kabul *22*F2, *42*C3
Kadesh *6*C2
Kadesia *33*D3
Kaffa (*mod.* Feodosiya)
   *42*A1, *52*D1, *72*C5
Kaffraria, *c.* 1900 *95*C2
Kaine *11*A3
Kairouan *57*C5
Kaiserswerth *38*B2
Kajana *70*E2
Kalach (Nimrud) *8*B1
Kalahari Desert *95*B1
Kalisz *67*E3
Kalka *42*B1
Kalmar *44*D2, *70*B4
Kalocsa *49*F4
Kama (river) *72*E3
Kamchatka *105*C-D1
Kamerun (Cameroon) *96*C4
Kammin (town) *44*D4, *70*B5
Kammin, Bishopric of, 1648 *67*D1
Kampen *61*D2
Kandahar *22*F3, *42*B4
Kanesh *6*B1
Kano *96*C4
Kansas, 1861–65 *92*C3
Kappel *48*C5
Karachi *97*B3
Karakorum *42*D2
Karbala *8*B4, *33*D3
Kardis *70*D3
Karelia
   1660 *70*E3   1725 *72*B3
Karikal *80*E5, *97*C5
Karlowitz (Karlovci)
   *71*E3, *76*E4

Karlsbad (Karlovy Vary)
   *86*C3, *91*C4
Karlshamn *73*B1
Karlskrona *70*B4, *76*D2
Karlsruhe *91*B4
Karlstad *70*B3
Karnak *2*B3
Kars *97*B2
Kashgar *42*C3
Kashmir
   1858 *80*D-E1
   1914 *97*C3
Kassel *73*A2, *91*B3
Kassites *6*E2
Katyn *104*D4
Kaufbeuren *67*C5
Kazan *72*D3
Kazan, Khanate of *72*D-E3–4
Keksgolm (county), 1660 *70*E2–3
Keksgolm (town) *70*E3
Kempten *67*C5
Kenilworth *51*C2
Kenninghall *62*C1
Kensington, London *66*A6
Kent *51*C3, *65*E4
Kentucky, 1861–65 *92*D3–4
Kenya, 1968 *108*B-C3
Kerbela *see* Karbala
Kerch *11*F1
Kerma *2*A5
Kesselsdorf *81*C4
Kharkov *72*C4
Khartoum *96*D4
Khiva *97*B2
Khorsabad *8*B1
Kiangsi *97*E3
Kiaochow *97*E2

Kiel *44*C4, *91*C1
Kiev *42*A1, *72*B4, *74*D5
Kilkenny *65*B4
Killiecrankie *65*C2
Kimberley *95*B1
Kings, Valley of the *2*A3, *5*
King's road, between
    Susa and Sardes *10*A-D2–4
Kinross *65*E1
Kinsai (*mod.* Hangchow) *42*F3
Kinshasa (Leopoldville)
    *108*B4
Kipr (Cyprus) *37*E5
Kirkholm *70*D4
Kirkuk *8*C2
Kish *8*C4
Kistna (*mod.* Krishna, river) *80*E4
Klara (river) *70*B3
Kobe *97*F2
Koblenz *38*B2
Koburg *63*D5
Kokenhusen *44*F2
Kolberg *44*D4, *82*D1
Kolin *82*D4
Komarov *100*F4
Königsberg *44*E3, *76*E2
Konya *60*D4
Korea, *c.* 1300 *42*F2
    1914 *97*F2
    1941–42 *105*B1
    1942–45 *106*B4
    1968 *108*E1
Kottbus *81*D3
Kotyora *24*C4
Kourland

1370 *44*E3   1660 *70*D4
1721 *76*E2   1795 *84*E1
1796 *72*A3   1812 *86*D1
Kovno *73*C1
Kragerø *70*A3
Krak *41*C3
Krakow *39*E3, *43*D2, *44*E5
Krakow, Republic of,
    1815 *87*C3
Krasnik *100*E3
Krefeld *82*B3
Kremsmünster *36*E5
Kringen *70*A2
Kronborg *70*A4
Kronstadt *72*B3
Kuban (province) *60*D2
Kuban (river) *72*C5
Kufa *33*E3
Kunersdorf *82*D2
Kura (river) *72*D-E6
Kurdistan *24*D5
Kurhesse *91*B-C3
Kuril Is. *97*F1, *105*C1
Kurisches Haff *100*E1
Kurna *2*B3
Kush (Nubia) *2*A-B5
Küstrin *81*D3
Kut *8*C4
Kutno *100*E3
Kuwait, 1914 *96*E3, *97*A3
    1919–35 *101*E2   1968 *107*F5
Kvikne *70*A2
Kwajalein *106*D6
Kweichow *97*E3
Kyffhäuser *39*D3

L

Labrador *58*B2
La Chapelle *1*A2
La Charité, Paris *83*A3
Lachish *9*D4
La Cité, Paris *83*B3
La Conciergerie, Paris *83*B2(5)
Laconia *14*B3
Lade *37*C1
Ladoga, Lake *70*E3
Ladrone (Mariana) Is. *58*F4
Ladysmith *95*C1
Laerdal *70*A2
Lagash *8*C5
Lagos *96*B4
La Grosse *59*C3
Lahore *97*C3
Laibach (*mod.* Ljubljana) *86*D4
Lake of the Woods *59*C3
La Madeleine, Paris *83*A1
La Mancha *55*C5
La Marche *62*C4
Lambaesis (*mod.* Lambèse) *29*B4
Lambeth, London *66*C6
Lamia *14*B2

Lampsacus (*mod.* Lapseki) *11*E2
Lancashire *65*D3
Lancaster (county) *51*B1
Lancaster (town) *51*B1
Landau *67*B4
Landsberg *64*E4
Landshut *82*D5
Langanes *37*A1
Langres *50*E1, *99*C5
Languedoc, 1429 *51*C-D6
    1562–92 *62*C-D4–5
Lanuvium (*mod.* Lanuvio) *25*E2
Laon *43*C2, *51*D3
La Orilla *59*B5
Laos
    1914 *97*E4   1968 *108*E2
La Paz *56*E4, *88*E3
Lapland *70*D1
La Rabida *55*A6
Larach *8*C4
Laredo *59*B4
Larisa *14*B2
La Rochelle *62*B3
Larsa *8*C5

M

Moab 9E5
Modena 45C2
Modena, Duchy of
　1454 45C2　　　　1701 71D4
　1721 76D4　　　　1815 87C4
　1859–60 89C2, 90B3
Modoc Indians 59A3
Modrusch 49E4
Møen 82C1
Moeris, Lake 2A2
Moesia, A.D. 117 29C3
Mogilev 73D2, 101D1
Mogul Empire 79A, B
Moguntiacum (mod. Mainz) 29B2
Mohacs 60B1, 76E4
Moldavia (river) 82D4
Moldavia
　1556 57E3　　　　1680 60C2
　1701 71F3　　　　1721 76F3–4
　1812 86E3　　　　1878 93C1
Molde 70A2
Mollwitz 81E4
Moluccas 58F4, 108F3
Mombasa 58D4, 96E5
Monaco (town) 85A2
Monaco, Principality of, 1860 90A3
　1914–18 98C3　　　1968 107B4
Mondovi 49C5, 85A2
Mongolia, c. 1300 42D-E2
　1914 97D-E2
　1941–42 105A1
Monreale 38D6, 43D5
Monrovia 96A4
Mons (Bergen) 68B5
Montana 92B2
Mont Cenis 25D1
Monte Alban 56A1
Monte Cassino 34B2, 43D4
Montenegro, 1520 60B2
　1701 71E4　　　　1721 76E5
　1812 86D4　　　　1878 93A-B2
　1912–13 94A-B5
　1914–18 98D4
　1919–35 101C2
Montereau 51D4
Montevideo 88E4
Montferrat, 1454 45A2
Montmartre, Paris 83B1
Montone (river) 35D1
Montpellier 43C4
Montreal 59D3, 92E2
Mont St Michel 43B2
Montu, Temple of 4
Monza 38B3
Moravia, 814 33B2
　843 36E4　　　　c. 900 37C3
　962 38E2　　　　1100 39D3
　1556 57D2　　　　1648 67E4
　1721 76D3　　　　1756–63 82E4
　1871 91D4　　　　1939 102D4
Moray 65C2
Moray Firth 65D1
Morea, 1556 57E5
　1701 71F5　　　　1721 76E6
　1812 86E5　　　　1878 93B3
　1912–13 94B-C6

Morgarten 48C5
Morges 48A6
Morocco
　814 33A4–5　　　c. 1600 58C3
　1812 86A5–6
　1914 96B3
　1914–18 98A-B4
　1919–35 101A2
　1939–45 104A6
　1968 108A2
Morotai 106B6
Mosa (mod. Maas or Meuse, river)
　27F1–2
Moscow 42B1, 72C3
Moscow, Principality of
　c. 1300 72C3
　Grand Duchy of, 1462 72C-D3–4
Mosel or Moselle (river)
　67B4, 99C2–4
Mosella (mod. Mosel or Moselle, river)
　27F2
Moslems in Europe, 1560 63
Moss 70B3
Mossel Bay 95B2
Mosul 33D3, 60E4
Moulins 62D3
Moutiers 49C4
Mozambique (state),
　1750 75D4
　1915 96D-E5–6
　1968 108B-C4–5
Mozambique (town) 58D4, 96E5
Mühlberg 57D2
Mühlhausen 57C2, 64C5, 67C3
Mukden (mod. Shenyang)
　97E2, 105B1
Mülhausen (Mulhouse)
　48B5, 64B6, 82B5
Mulhouse 82B5
Münchengrätz 91D4
Munda 28A3
Munich 76D4
Munster 65A4
Münster 44B5, 67B3
Münster, Bishopric of
　1648 67B3
Murat 62C4
Murcia 55D6
Murmansk 103D1
Murray 65E1
Muscat 97B3
Muscat and Oman 108C2
Mussolini, conquests of
　1935–39 102
Mut, Temple of 4
Mutina (mod. Modena) 23B1
Mycale, Mt. 20D4
Mycenae 14B3, 15B6
Mycerinus, pyramid of 3
Myconos 14D3
Mylae 16C2, 25F4
Myriandrus 11F3, 24C5
Mysia 26A2
Mysore 79A5, 80D-E4
Mytilene 14E2, 21F2
Mytistratum 16C2

New Hebrides *105*D3, *106*D6
New Holland (Australia) *58*F5
Newington, London *66*C6
New Jersey
   1783 *78*E2–3   1861–65 *92*E3
New Karleby *70*D2
New Mexico, 1912 *92*B4
New Orleans *59*C4, *78*D4, *92*D5
New Sweden *77*A1
New York (state)
   1783 *78*E2   1861–65 *92*E2
New York (town) *77*B1, *78*E2, *92*E3
New Zealand *75*F5
Nez Perce Indians *59*A-B3
Niaux *1*A2
Nicaea, Asia Minor
   *29*D3, *39*F5, *43*F4
Nicaea (*mod.* Nice) *11*C2, *23*A1
Nicaea, Empire of *40*E3
Nicaragua *56*C2
Nice *36*C5, *90*A3
Nice, County of, 1859–60 *90*A3
Nicephorium *22*C2
Nicobar Is., 1849–1914 *97*D5
Nicolet, route of *59*C3
Nicomedia *20*E1
Nicopolis *53*B4
Nicosia *107*D5
Niemen (river) *70*D4
Nieuport *68*A4, *99*A1
Niger (river) *96*A-B4
Niger (state) *108*A-B2–3
Nigeria
   1914 *96*B-C4   1968 *108*A-B3
Nijmegen *68*C3
Nike, sanctuary of
   Acropolis, Athens *13*
Nike, Paeonius's statue of
   Olympia *18*C2
Nike, statue of, Delphi *19*D4
Nike, Temple of
   Acropolis, Athens *17*B4
Nikolsburg *97*D5
Nile (river) *2*, *96*D3–4
Nilus (*mod.* Nile, river) *28*D5
Nîmes *36*B5
Nimrud *8*B1
Nine Elms, London *66*B6
Nineveh *6*D2, *8*B1, *24*D5
Nipigon, Lake *59*C3
Nippur *8*C4
Nish *32*D4, *76*E5
Nizam, dominions of the
   1858 *80*E3–4
   1914 *97*C4
Nizhni-Novgorod (*mod.* Gorki) *72*D3
Noli *49*C5
Nordhausen *67*C3
Nördlingen *64*C6, *67*C4, *81*C5
Nordmark *38*C-D1
Noreia (*mod.* Neumark) *28*C2
Norfolk *65*E4
Noricum (Roman province) *29*B-C2
Normandy
   c. 900 *37*B3   1100 *39*B3
   1180–1453 *50*   1429 *51*B-C3

Normans, Kingdom of the, 1154 *38*
Norrköping *70*C3
North America
   c. 1600 *58*   1650–1763 *77*
   1750 *75*   1783 *78*
   1783–1912 *92*
   1861–65 (Civil War) *92*
North Borneo, 1914 *97*E-F5
North Bukovina *103*C2
North Cape *72*B1
North Carolina
   1783 *78*E3
   1861–65 *92*E4
North Dakota, 1889 *92*C2
Northeastern Europe, 1660 *70*
Northern Rhodesia *see* Zambia
Northern States, 1861–65 *92*
North German Confederation
   1886–71 *91*
North Korea *108*E1
North Schleswig *101*B1
North Sea *76*C2
Northumberland *51*C1
North Vietnam *108*E2
North Wales *36*A4
Northwest Greeks
   (North Dorians) *14*
Norton Sound *59*B1
Norvasund (Strait of Gibraltar) *37*A5
Norway, *c.* 900 *37*C1
   1370 *44*B-C1–2
   1815 *87*B-C1
   1914–18 *98*C1   1919–35 *101*B1
   1939–41 *103*B-C1
   1942–45 *104*C4
   1968 *107*B1–2
   See also Denmark for the
   period 1397–1814
Norwich *65*E4
Nöteborg *70*E3, *72*C3
Notre Dame, Paris *83*B3
Nottingham (county) *65*D-E3
Nottingham (town) *65*E4
Novara *89*A2
Nova Scotia
   1650–1763 *77*   1783 *78*F1
   1783–1912 *92*F2
Novaya Zemlya *58*D1
Novgorod (town) *44*F1, *72*B3
Novgorod, Republic of
   1370 *44*F1–2
   1462–1605 *72*B-C3
Novi *85*A2
Noyon *49*B3, *62*D2
Nubia *2*A-B5
Numantia
   (*mod.* Cerro de Garray) *25*B2
Numidia, during Punic Wars *25*D5
   44 B.C. *28*B-C4
   A.D. 117 *29*B4
Nuremberg *38*C2, *67*C4
Nursia *35*E2
Nyasa, Lake *96*D5
Nyasaland *see* Malawi
Nyslott *70*E2
Nystad *76*E1

O

Oaxaca *56*B1
Ob (river) *42*C1
Oceanus Atlanticus
    (Atlantic Ocean) *29*A1–2
Oceanus Britannicus *28*A-B1
Oder (river) *67*D-E2–3
Odessa *86*E3
Oeta, Mt. *14*B2
Ofen (Buda) *84*D5
Ohio (river) *78*D3
Ohio (state) *92*D3
Oise (river) *99*B3
Oka (river) *72*D3
Okinawa *106*B5
Oklahoma *92*C4
Öland
    1370 *44*D3   1660 *70*B4
Olbia, Sardinia *25*E3
Olbia, on Black Sea *11*E1
Oldenburg, 1648 *67*B2
    1815 *87*B2   1871 *91*B2
Old Karleby *70*D2
Old Sarum *86*B2
Old Spanish Trail *59*A-C3
Oliva *81*E2
Olmütz *82*E4
Oloron *49*A5
Olympia *14*B3, *18*
Olympus, Mt. *14*B1
Olynthus *14*C1
Omaha *92*C3
Oman
    814 *33*F3   1914 *97*B3–4
Ombos *2*B3
Ombrone (river) *35*D2
Omdurman *96*D4
Onega (river) *72*C2
Onega, Lake *72*C3
Ontario, Lake *59*D3, *78*E2
Oporto *39*A4, *55*A5, *86*A4
Oradea Mare (Grosswardein) *49*F3
Oran *32*A5
Orange (river) *95*A-C1–2
Orange (town) *43*C4; *69*E4
Orange, Principality of *69*E4
Orange Free State, *95*C1–2, *96*D6
Orbetello *85*B3
Orchomenus *15*B5
Örebro *70*B3
Oregon *92*A2
Oregon City *59*A3

Oregon Trail *59*B-C3
Öreting *37*C1
Orissa *80*E-F3
Orkney Is.
    c. 900 *37*B1   1370 *44*A1
    1914–18 *98*B1   1968 *107*B2
Orléanais *69*D-E2
Orléans (province) *51*C-D4
Orléans (town) *37*B3, *43*B3
Ormuz *42*B4, *58*D3
Orontes (river) *41*C2–4
Ortospana (mod. Kabul) *22*F2
Orvieto *45*D3
Osaka *97*F2
Oseberg *37*C1
Ösel, 1100 *39*E1
    1370 *44*E2   1660 *70*D3
    1725 *72*A3   1914–18 *98*D1
Oslo *44*C1, *103*C1
Osnabrück *44*B4, *67*B2
Osnabrück, Bishopric of
    1648 *67*B2
Osrhoene (Roman province) *29*E4
Ossa, Mt. *14*B1
Ossero *49*E5
Ostend *61*A3
Österbotten *70*D2
Ostia *35*D3
Ostmark *38*D3
Ostrogoths *32*E2
Ostrogoths, Kingdom of the
    526 *32*C-D3–5
Ostrolenka *91*E2
Otchakov *73*E3
Otranto *76*E5
Ottawa (river) *78*E1
Ottawa Indians *59*C-D3
Ottoman Empire, 1355 *53*C5
    1355–1680 *60*
    1556 *57*D-F3–5
    1701 *71*E-F2–5
    1721 *76*E-F4–6
    1812 *86*D-F3–5
    1815 *87*C4
    See also Turkey
Oudenarde *71*C2
Oudh
    1858 *80*E2   1914 *97*C3
Overijssel *61*E2
Oxford *43*B2, *65*D4
Oxus (river) *22*E2

P

Pacific Ocean, during Second
    World War, *105*, *106*
Pacific Railway
    Chicago-San Francisco *92*A-D3
    Montreal-Vancouver *92*A-E1–2
Paderborn *36*C4
Paderborn, Bishopric of
    1648 *67*C3   1756–63 *82*B3

Padua *43*C3, *45*D2
Padus (mod. Po, river) *25*E1
Paestum (Posidonia) *23*D2
Pakistan *108*C-D2
Palaeolithic sites *1*
Palaestra, Olympia *18*A1–2
Palais Bourbon, Paris *83*A2
Palais de Justice, Paris *83*B2(5)

Q

Romulus, Temple of, Rome *31*C6(12)
Roncaglia *39*C4
Roncesvalles *33*A3, *36*A6
Rǿros *70*B2
Rosendal *70*A3
Rosetta *2*A1
Rosheim *69*F2
Roskilde *43*C1, *70*A4
Rossbach *82*C3
Ross River *59*B2
Rostock *43*C1, *44*C4
Rostra, Rome *31*B6(2)
Rothenburg *64*C6, *67*C4
Rotomagus (*mod.* Rouen) *27*E2
Rotterdam *61*C3
Rottweil *67*C5
Rouen *43*B2, *51*C3
Roussillon *69*E5
Rovno *100*F4
Ruanda-Urundi
  see Rwanda and Burundi
Rubico (river) *23*C1
Rüdesheim *39*C3
Rue de Sève, Paris *83*A3
Rue St Denis, Paris *83*B2
Rue St Honoré, Paris *83*A-B1–2
Rue St Jacques, Paris *83*B3

Rue St Martin, Paris *83*B2
Rügen
  1370 *44*C4   1648 *67*D1
  1660 *70*B4   1721 *76*D2
  1756–63 *82*D1   1865 *91*C1
Rügenwalde *44*D3, *81*D2
Ruhr (river) *68*C4
Ruhr Area *102*C4
Rumelia
  1721 *76*F5   1812 *86*E4
Rusaddir (*mod.* Melilla) *25*B5
Russia, 900 *37*D2
  1300–1825 *72*   1721 *76*E-F1–3
  c. 1750 *75*D-F1–2
  1800–1914 (in Asia) *97*
  1812 *86*D-F1–2
  1815 *87*C-D1–2
  1871 *91*E-F1–3
  1914–18 *98*D-F1–3
  See also Soviet Union
Russian Principalities, 1100 *39*
Ruthenia *102*E4
Rütli *48*C5
Rwanda *108*B4
Ryukyu Is.
  1914 *97*F3
  1942–45 *106*B5

S

Saale (river) *44*C5
Saar
  1935 *102*C4   1968 *107*B3
Saarbrücken *91*B4
Sabini *23*C2
Sacramento *59*A3, *92*A3
Sadowa *91*D4
Sagres *55*A6
Saguntum (*mod.* Sagunto) *25*C3
Sahara Desert *96*B3
St Andrews *65*E1
St Asaph *49*A1
St Augustine *78*E4
St Bernard *48*B6
St Bernard, Great *85*A1
St Bernard, Little *25*D1
St Bertrand *49*B5
St Brieuc *49*A3
Saint Cloud *86*B3
St Davids *49*A1
Saint Denis *43*B2, *51*C4
Sainte Chapelle, Paris *83*B2(5)
Saintes *49*B4
St Flour *49*B4
St Gallen *43*C3, *48*D5
Saint Geneviève (Pantheon)
  Paris *83*B4
St Germain *62*C2
Saint Germain des Prés
  Paris *83*B3
St Gildas de Ruis *43*B3
St Gotthard *48*C6

St Helena
  c. 1750 *75*C4
  1945 *108*A4
St Lawrence (river) *59*D3, *78*E-F1
St Lawrence, Gulf of *78*F1
St Louis *59*C3, *78*D3, *92*D3
St Malo *49*A3
St Mihiel *99*C4
St Omer *61*A4
St Paul, Minnesota *92*C2
St Paul's, London *66*C6
St Petersburg (Leningrad)
  *72*B3, *76*E1, *101*C1
St Pol de Léon *49*A3
St Pons *49*B5
St Quentin *61*B5, *62*D2
St Roche, Paris *83*B2(4)
St Thomas *75*B3
St Victor, Paris *83*C4
Saipan *106*C5
Sais *2*A1
Sakhalin, 1914 *97*F1
  1941–45 *105*C1, *106*C4
Sakjegözü *6*C2
Sakkara *2*A1
Salado (river) *56*E5
Salamanca *43*A4, *55*B5
Salamis (island) *15*C6
Salamis (town) *15*C6
Salef (river) *40*F4, *41*A2
Salerno *34*B2, *43*D4
Salerno, Principality of *38*D5

T

W

Warka *8*C5
Warsaw *73*C2, *74*B5, *103*C2, *104*C5
Warsaw, Grand Duchy of
   1812 *86*D2–3
Warta (river) *82*E2
Wartburg *39*D3
Warwick (county) *51*B-C2
Warwick (town) *51*B2
Washington (state), 1889 *92*A1–2
Washington (town) *92*E3, F4
Waterford *37*B2
Waterloo *86*C3
Wearmouth *43*B1
Weichsel *see* Vistula
Weihaiwei *97*E2
Weimar *64*D5, *102*D4
Weinsberg *39*C3
Weissenburg *91*B4
Wellington, expedition to Spain
   1808–9 *86*
Wells, England *49*A2
Wells, U.S.A. *59*C3
Wenden *70*D4
Wendland *36*D4
Werben *64*D4
Weser (river) *81*B2–4
Wessex, 526 *32*B2
Western Dvina (river) *70*D-E4
Western Front, 1914–18 *99*
Western Powers, 1939 *103*
West Frankish Kingdom
   c. 900 *37*B3–4
West Frisian Is. *68*B-C1
West Indies, *c.* 1600 *58*A-B3
West Irian
   (formerly Dutch New Guinea)
   *108*F3
Westminster, London *66*B6
Westminster Abbey, London *66*B6
Westmorland *65*D3
Westphalia
   c. 1630 *64*C5   1648 *67*B3
   1812 *86*C2   1865 *91*B3
West Prussia
   13th and 14th centuries *74*A4
   1756–63 *82*E1   1772 *81*E2
   1865 *91*E2
   1919–35 *101*C1
West Turkestan, 1914 *97*B-C2

West Virginia *92*D-E3
West Wales *36*A4
Wetzlar *44*B5, *67*C3
Wexford *65*B4
Whitby *32*B1
Whitechapel, London *66*D6
Whitehall, London *66*C6
White Mountain *64*E5
White Russia, 1772 *84*F2
White Sea *72*C2
Wieliczka *74*B5
Wiener-Neustadt *49*E3
Wiesbaden *102*D4
Wight, Isle of *39*B3, *65*D5
Wilderness *92*F4
Wildhaus *48*D5
Wilhelmshöhe *91*B3
Wilhelmsthal *82*C3
Willendorf *1*A2
Wiltshire *51*B3
Winchester *43*B2, *49*B2
Windau *44*E2
Windsor *51*C2
Winnipeg, Lake *59*C3
Winterthur *48*D5
Wisconsin (river) *78*D1–2
Wisconsin (state) *92*C-D2
Wismar *70*A5, *82*C1
Wittenberg *57*C2, *64*D5
Witwatersrand *95*C1
Wolfenbüttel *64*C5
Wollgast *81*D2
Worcester (county) *51*B2
Worcester (town) *39*B2, *65*D4
Worms *38*B2, *43*C2, *67*C4
Wörth *91*B4
Wounded Knee *59*B3
Wroxeter *36*B4
Württemberg *38*B2
Württemberg, Duchy of
   1648 *67*C4–5
Württemberg, Kingdom of
   1812 *86*C3   1815 *87*B-C3
   1871 *91*B-C4–5
Würzburg *43*C2
Würzburg, Bishopric of
   1648 *67*C4
Wüsterhausen *81*D3
Wyoming *92*B2–3

X

Xerxes' Canal
   *20*C1

Xerxes' expedition against Greece
   480 B.C. *20*

Y

Yalta *104*E5
Yanaon *80*E4, *97*C4

Yangtse-kiang (river) *97*D-E3
Yarmouth *44*A4